This is a brilliant book with many valuable insights into the most complex but unexplored topic — how to manage your boss. It not only explodes a number of myths and assumptions but also offers practical tools and suggestions to deal with difficult situations — BLASTS is one such example. That, by itself, is worth the price of this book!

—*K Murali, Director, Human Resources, GE, India*

"*Boss is always right*" is not true. "*Boss is mostly wrong and root cause of my problem*" is how most people see him. In this excellent book Rashmi Datt has put the issue in the proper perspective. An important must read for every young person starting a career, as well as for all those struggling to make it a success, as we are all dreaming to make (team) India Inc a global powerhouse in the next 20 years.

—*Narendra K. Dhand, Chairman and Managing Director, Micromatic Grinding Technologies Ltd*

An excellent guide to managing yourself and your career in any work environment, whether corporate, academics or any other. It shows you how to take responsibility instead of blaming others or leaving things to fate.

—*Sudhir K. Jain, Professor, Department of Civil Engineering, IIT, Kanpur*

Contains very useful tips on surviving the workplace pressure-cooker.

—*Rachna Mukherjee, HR Director, Daksh, an IBM subsidiary*

Brilliant. It's about time someone touched upon this subject given that it has so much relevance to our times and so much impact on the overall productivity of any organisation. A must read for subordinates and bosses.

—Ashuthosh Khanna, Chief Operating Officer,
Grey Worldwide (India)

Provides a fresh perspective on boss-subordinate relationships and gives simple, usable solutions for seemingly complex problems. Useful not just for subordinates (who may or may not be having boss problems), but also for bosses! It provides valuable insights on how a subordinate may be viewing his boss.

—Nidhi Sekhar, Vice President, Human Resources,
Citifinancial, India

About the Author

A post-graduate in management from BITS, Pilani, Rashmi Datt has 19 years of experience in training and HRD. She worked for eight years with Pfizer, Mumbai before starting Dialog, a learning services delivery consultancy. She conducts workshops in India and abroad focusing on individual and organisational growth and enabling participants to identify and change dysfunctional behaviour patterns—the way we relate, interact, deal with conflict, or utilise resources. Participants take away not just insights, but concrete skills and practical steps that they can implement in their lives from day one. She is a qualified MBTI trainer from the Association for Psychological Type (APT), USA. She can be contacted at : rashmi_dialog@yahoo.com.

Gender Mender

The work world surely has bosses of both sexes. In this book we have referred to the boss as a "he" merely for the sake of keeping the text easy to read and avoiding the cumbersome use of "he or she" at every reference.

managing your BOSS

RASHMI DATT

ILLUSTRATIONS BY
DEB DULAL DUTTA

First published 2005
Reprinted 2006, 2018

ISBN 978-81-8328-000-6

Published by
Wisdom Tree
4779/23, Ansari Road
Darya Ganj, Delhi 110002
Ph.: 011-23247966/67/68
wisdomtreebooks@gmail.com

Printed in India

To my parents…

Acknowledgements

In the course of my workshops I have met hundreds of participants who have shared their frustrations and workplace difficulties, from where many of the case studies have been taken. I would like to thank them for enriching the workshops, enlightening me and for providing inspiration to write this book. I am also grateful to the many middle- and senior-level managers who agreed to be interviewed and share their work experiences on the condition of anonymity.

However, I owe special thanks to:

Shobit Arya of Wisdom Tree, without whose patience and encouragement this book would not have been written; S.K. Dujari for taking the trouble of going through the very first draft and providing invaluable inputs and comments, which have helped shape the book in its final form; Rear Admiral P.N. Gour who provided insights, feedback and shared very useful experiences in the course of the writing of this book.

I am also indebted to N. Narasimhan, Puneet Aneja, Nidhi Datt and Sudhanshu Datt for their support and suggestions.

I must also thank Deb Dutta, the illustrator of this book, who worked in perfect synchronisation to produce these lively drawings.

And last but not least, I would like to express my gratitude to Ajay Jacob who helped with the text and provided enormous support in many other ways.

Preface

In the course of my workshops on enhancing personal effectiveness at the workplace, when we discuss workplace issues, or communication in frustrating and difficult situations, I have so often experienced despondency, helplessness and even anger, "But what can I do with a boss like this?"

Four years ago when a training manager asked me to include a session on 'Boss Management' in a three-day workshop on 'Personal Effectiveness', I jumped at the idea. I thought it was a bold and wise thought, because management normally shies away from this topic. Isn't it a strange anomaly that leadership skills are drummed and dinned into managers to sway employees to produce more, to want to work better and harder...but what about followership? The art of working effectively and harmoniously with superiors?

Strangely enough, it is assumed that it will happen innately and automatically. The 'managed' doesn't even realise he has an active (and not a passive) role to play for the partnership to be successful! It's ironic that everyone in an organisation doesn't even reach headship position; on the other hand, followership is a skill everyone needs.

One reason why management avoids this subject is that it fears the potential of being manipulated/ manoeuvred. But isn't it a reflection of senior management's own insecurities—it is okay to empower managers to manage downwards, but to manage upwards... no no, we don't want employees to become too smart! In reality, both the organisation and the individual will benefit by enabling the employee with the awareness and skill of being proactive rather than reactive.

Interestingly enough, the reaction of participants is often mixed when this subject is discussed in a group. I remember a person's comment at the end of the session, "I am feeling uneasy, like after a large and heavy meal. In my 20 years of work experience I have never even given this subject a thought… have I missed out on something?" Many are deeply appreciative… "It has opened my eyes to perspectives and insights that I didn't know existed…"

I hope that as you read this book, you will also gain valuable insights and practical tips to develop a constructive and proactive approach to managing this important relationship. If it cannot help you solve your problems, it will certainly tell you where you are going wrong. After you read this book I would love to hear your reactions, feedback and experiences on this subject.

Rashmi Datt
rashmi_dialog@yahoo.com

Contents

What is this boss management all about?

Why do I Need to Manage My Boss?

Why do I need to 'manage' my boss? Isn't that apple-polishing, or to put it more bluntly, sucking up? Isn't the story of success about working hard and producing results, rather than assuaging the boss's ego? If my work is good enough, shouldn't that speak for itself—so why should I need to resort to political manoeuvring of this kind?

Moreover, who am I to manage the boss? It would be highly presumptuous of me, for after all, he is my superior, with more wisdom, experience and skills. He is supposed to manage me; that's *his* job. He would take offence at the very idea that I might want or attempt to 'manage' him.

Sure, these are valid questions and doubts (if they are coming up in your mind) on the subject of upward management. To find answers, let's do a reality check of any work environment—corporate (both public and private sector), universities, schools, hospitals, non-profit organisations—anywhere.

Negativity at workplace is a fact of life

Which predominant emotion is felt by employees at work? What is your own frame of mind as you return home after a typical day's work? Your colleagues and friends—how do they feel? In the last one or two years, studies have been conducted which quantify emotional feelings of employees to their jobs. (Study conducted in September 2002 by Towers Perin in partnership with Gang and Gang over 1,100 employees in North America.) The results are not surprising: more than 50 per cent feel the negative emotion, and 33 per cent feel intensely negative about their work. Obviously there is a gap between employees' current and ideal work experiences.

Fears and pressure at work arise from a combination of many things: an excessive work-load (or conversely, lack of challenge resulting in boredom), indifferent recognition, and a concern for pay not being commensurate with performance. Most of the unhappiness gets concentrated in the boss-subordinate relationship, as for any employee, his boss is the face of the organisation. The outlet takes the form of sour and cutting comments at the office water-cooler or for that matter, family dinner-table, about bosses who are stupid, meddlesome, indecisive, unreasonable, unstable, ruthless, credit grabbing and arrogant slave drivers. (Have you heard discussions about bosses who are aware and enlightened, who provide support and encouragement, take timely action and understand the need for change?)

The consequences? Not only is there stress and unhappiness at the personal level, the organisation also loses heavily because of lowered morales, reduced productivity and half-hearted commitment. Surely there are alternatives and solutions?

The relationship with the boss needs to be cultivated.

The boss-subordinate relationship is complex

At the workplace we have to contend with many equations—with peers, seniors, juniors, suppliers and customers. Of these, the boss-subordinate association is one of the most vital and sensitive, yet the average employee makes little effort to managing it proactively. In fact the case more often than not is that it is mismanaged, with the boss put into the category of the 'enemy', or alternatively viewed as a game or a strategy where he has to be 'outwitted'!

Viewed objectively, it's an important relationship, which has to be cultivated. With anyone else (be it the parent, spouse, friend, or customer) we understand perfectly well, that to create a rapport requires patience, effort and a high degree of broadmindedness. We instinctively understand and follow Norman Vincent Peal's timeless priniciple—'show genuine interest in the other, and build bridges of trust and openness.'

The boss represents power, control and authority.

Yet when it comes to maintaining goodwill with the boss, we balk. Why is this equation fraught with many emotional overtones and undertones, assumptions and biases?

There are two main reasons. One is the representation the boss holds for me—of power, control and authority. Outwardly and rationally I accept the truth of organisational hierarchy, which entails that the boss 'controls' resources, and holds power over my plans, ideas, projects, strategies I may want to implement, including my appraisal and reward at year end. The need for control is inherent in all humans—the boss exercising it has greater legitimacy (as he sees it!). But it is not something I accept so willingly. Deep in the recesses of my mind and heart lurk feelings of resentment and anger (perhaps unknown even to me). According to psychiatrists, we react to authority figures somewhere in between the two extremes of *rebelliousness* ("He knows nothing, for heaven's sake!") and *blind acceptance* that comes from intimidation ("The all-wise and all-knowing boss knows best"). Which of these two are helpful or appropriate? Neither, for both you and the organisation.

So part of the dynamics of the equation is how *you* tend to respond to being managed—an aspect not explored or examined to the extent it deserves. So while we have been busy complaining and griping about the boss with the conviction that he is the source of all my miseries, there is a need for a ruthlessly honest self-examination of the other side of the coin—*my* contribution to the problem.

We get entangled in our own ego

The second reason is that in addition to this confusion of where to react from—rebelliousness or blind acceptance, we also get entangled in our own ego of an unspoken challenge, 'If you are my boss, prove to me your wisdom and maturity by taking the onus of the relationship.' In this faulty conclusion lies another erroneous thought: 'Boss's sagacity and astuteness should be as endless and deep as the ocean.'

Did you notice a dangerous word that has crept into our self-talk? The word 'should' results in a lot of heartburn, because we are establishing a difference between reality and the ideal. The ideal is a creation of our own mind, while the reality is real and present, which has to be coped with. The boss is a larger than life figure we have created. In actuality, he is far from an all-wise parent—he is a human being with his own foibles, limitations, idiosyncrasies, unfulfilled needs and wants. And that's how we should treat him: accepting his shortcomings as well as abilites, rather than first set up all the 'shoulds', then feel a grim satisfaction every time we discover new chinks in his armour.

Beware of the 'shoulds'

When we set up 'shoulds' in our mind, we are negating reality. Other 'shoulds' we become victims to are:

- **My boss *should* always have enough time for me.** Reality: The boss has a myraid other issues, problems and relationships to cope with. The time you get is more than you need. Plan and use it well.
- **The boss *should* spell out his expectations explicitly and in great detail.** Wrong again: It's your responsibility to ensure clarity by asking, cajoling, or extracting it out.
- **The boss *should* care about me, my growth and development.** It's a harsh reality, but what the boss really cares about are the results you produce and the work you deliver. So everytime you whine about job enrichment, foreign training, or the missed promotion, ask yourself how you are contributing to help him reach his goals.

The list is endless: he *should* ensure I have adequate resources, *should* not overburden me, *should* ensure I have reasonable deadlines, *should* get the best from me by tapping my potential, *should* keep me informed, etc, etc.

Why should he? To make an exaggerated point, do you have a whip that you can hold over him, ensuring that he complies with your 'shoulds'? You don't. So learn to understand and accept the boss as he is, instead of allowing the ego to get a kick out of pointing out faults and shortcomings.

Followership skills are underestimated

Endless material (books, training workshops, seminars and studies) are being churned out about leadership skills—to motivate employees to produce more, to want to work better and harder. But followership—the art of working effectively and harmoniously with superiors is assumed to 'just' happen.

Leaders will acknowledge that effectiveness of subordinates is not necessarily measured by levels of brightness, analytical skills, or brilliant strategies. What is equally, or more important, is the ability to collaborate, stay open and not get stuck in rigid ideas, the ability to support and at times, challenge decisions; of course, the bottom line being to deliver consistent results for the organisation's best. *So managing up is really about building an effective and productive relationship with the boss for the good of you, your boss and your organisation.*

What this book is about

The book does not claim to provide all the answers to your questions or problems in the form of a magic wand. What it does is to:

1. Draw your awareness to the fact that you do have a choice. The selection is between simply playing out a role in a drama scribbled (handed) by life, and on the other hand, writing out your own role, including some of the scripts, dialogues, movements, actions, reactions and emotions.
2. Help you analyse and understand your own personality as your unconscious attitudes and assumptions can lead to blocked mindsets. Greater awareness and acceptance of these can lead to a paradigm shift in perspectives and insights. This will result in a constructive approach more likely to get you positive results.
3. Understand the boss's personality, by studying his qualities, traits, requirements, tactics, quirks, eccentricities (who doesn't have them?), and work around that, instead of crying, "Why can't my boss be:
   - like me / like my ex-boss
   - more appreciative
   - more enterprising

- more considerate
- more communicative
- less rigid... (the list is endless).

Different bosses have different needs and styles of working (including managing time), so would it not be intelligent to adopt their approach, instead of (foolishly) insisting on mine?

4. Emphasise the importance and skills of upward communication. The mistake most of us make is to under-communicate about our own challenges, problems, opportunities, results and the need for the boss's support. The boss is not a mind reader, and bridges of communication have to be consciously built and maintained. Even if the boss forgets, or doesn't keep his commitments, it's my job to follow up.
5. Understand how to establish a solid relationship based on the strength of a professional reputation of delivering consistent and quality results.
6. Realise that it is important not just to be competent, but also to be perceived as competent. You could be putting in those extra hours of work, taking a lot of initiative in upgrading those quality standards, setting up new processes and systems, but you need to step out of your cubicle. In other words, it is also your job to sell—both your ideas and yourself (see 'The Story of Muthuswamy' below). Many of us mistakenly believe that if I present a fantastic idea to the boss, its value should be as clear as a bell. Why doesn't he grab it instead of dismissing it off? Successful managers have learnt the art of presenting the matter in the right context and light. They have also learnt the art of getting noticed and rewarded.

Lessons from the story of Muthuswamy

The story of Muthuswamy* is common enough.

Fifteen years ago, he started life in earnest. With a bright academic record and parents' blessings behind him, he was all set

* Muthuswamy is an *Accounts Assistant Manager* at a large multinational pharmaceutical company in Mumbai.

Muthuswamy believed that 'my work should speak for itself'.

to start what appeared to be a promising career. He had no other thought in mind—expect to work hard, prove his worth, make an honest living, and rise up the ladder of life. He followed all his father's advice of giving his job long hours, loyalty and utmost dedication. But today he lives his life with disillusionment and bitterness as he feels he hasn't got his due recognition.

Where did things go wrong? He went that extra mile, performed good quality work, and was known in his department as a reliable batter. He would work long hours without complaining to meet an urgent deadline. BUT, whenever it came to the question of that promotion, or foreign posting, or a juicy project, it somehow just slipped Muthuswamy by.

In other words, he was a workhorse who was taken for granted. During his fifteen years of work, he hardly ever spoke up at meetings (unless a remark was addressed to him), never voiced to any of his bosses his real feelings (about fair or unfair treatment), and made almost no effort in networking with other seniors or his boss's bosses. 'My work should speak for itself,' had been his motto. Strangely, he had followed in the footsteps of his father whose career had also stagnated at the middle level. Do you know of such a Muthuswamy?

Do you see that it is not about "his boss should have..." but rather Muthuswamy's (and all of ours) responsibility towards creating a greater impact at the workplace? As we network with seniors, peers and juniors, enhance our image, become more assertive and self-confident, we are actually becoming more effective at our work. Our resourcefulness increases, and with it our ability to influence, persuade, get things done and drive change.

Another myth laid to rest is, *'If I work hard, I will automatically be rewarded'*. The formula of 'automatic rewards' perhaps held good during school and college life. Conscientious and sincere effort in academics led to doing (reasonably) well in examinations, which in turn led to being moved or promoted to the next level, which was repeated year after year. It was a simple equation, with hardly any other variables playing a role of any consequence.

However, the real world is much more complex. While this equation is not invalid, there are many more rules, axioms, theorems and variables we need to keep track of, which this book aims to discuss. Many competent executives devote much time and energy in managing subordinates, products, technologies, markets, and changing government policies, but are extremely passive when it comes to managing their bosses, to their own detriment.

To be able to 'manage' this situation requires maturity, immense patience and a relentless watch over your own actions and behaviour. If you decide the rewards of greater self-satisfaction, self-confidence and sense of control over your life are worthwhile, then read on! In the words of Peter Drucker: "*You don't have to like and admire your boss, nor do you have to hate him. You do have to manage him, however, so that he becomes your resource for achievement, accomplishment... and personal success as well.*"

2

Bosses are Bosses: What Kind of Subordinate are You?

My response to the boss depends upon my self-esteem

Bosses come in all shapes and sizes. They have their own personalities, perceptions, needs, biases, competencies and incompetencies. In our mind we set up our own window from which we view them, little realising that our mindsets and expectations also play a huge role in setting the tone and colour of this relationship. So the story is not just about the boss and his personality quirks, as much it's about our own self-esteem, our own anxieties and our own life history.

A lot of our feeling of self-worth and self-esteem today dates back to childhood experiences of dealing with parents, teachers, older relatives, who held a lot of power over us—the power of criticism. The child's mind could not make out the difference between a wrong or naughty *act* and *being* wrong or bad. A reprimand from these authority figures left feelings of 'not okay' inside us. Our mind was unable (then) to differentiate between corrective (objective) feedback for a specific act or deed and the entire person being rejected or labelled as worthless.

As adults, our workplace is a re-creation of the past (childhood) situations as it is replete with power figures, hierarchies, rules and regulations. We continue to carry these internal (irrational) associations and unconsciously give the bosses a larger than life hold over our minds. When there is a negative trigger with the boss withholding resources or shooting a proposal down (denial), or pushing deadlines and targets (control), or giving negative feedback (reprimand), we are flooded by old recordings of unhealthy feelings. These can be of rage and ire (I'll show him), or on the other hand, of rejection and helpless resignation. To cope, we take a stance somewhere in between the two extremes of *rebellion* (rejection) or *compliance* (blind acceptance).

It's possible that our reactions may have been different had we met with similar responses vis-à-vis a colleague, subordinate or friend! So there is a need to examine our responses:

- Where are they coming from? (What was my relationship with my father and mother? Were there elements of rebellion or compliance in it?)
- Are they appropriate to the situation (today) or are they an over-reaction?
- If I examine my history of relationships with previous bosses, can I identify a pattern—is there a tendency towards either rebellion or compliance?

Our reactions to bosses fall between two extremes: Rebellion or compliance

"***You are not the boss of me. I am the boss of me***"**—a rebellious response.**

According to Leonard Schlesinger, earlier professor at Harvard Business School and author of *The Real Heroes of Business... and*

One extreme of our reaction to bosses : Compliance.

not a CEO among Them: "Most of us work in hierarchical organisations—and we have bosses. Therefore the consequences are grave when you establish a mindset that says, 'You are not the boss of me. I am the boss of me'."

In other words, in relating with authority figures, we are reacting in a rebellious way. When confronted with doing something I don't want to do, or when someone is trying to control me, my rejoinder becomes:

- "It's my way or no way."
- I join the underground resistance—"I won't get mad, I'll get even some day."

The other extreme of our reaction to bosses : Rebelliousness.

- "What an idiot! Can't he see the value in what I'm saying?"
- "He has no business instructing me on how I should divide responsibilities in my team."

So the pulse sent off is, 'Hey, if you are the boss of me, you have to prove yourself worthy of my respect by being smarter, wiser and cleverer than me; which you are not, so how can I respect you?' Without doubt, the boss picks up the pulse, and his stand changes from dislike, to distrust, to outright hostility. Negativity on either side grows and feeds on each other.

"*The boss knows best*": Over-compliant response

At the other end of the continuum is compliance, easily giving power away. This passive stand is characterised by:

- Ingratiating myself by always agreeing with the boss; paying excess deference.
- Treating the boss like a father figure.
- Not making any effort to offer a contrary view, to question a decision even in situations where it would be desirable (and possible) to reverse a decision.
- "The boss has said so, and so it must be."

It is possible to re-programme and change these old response patterns. In other words, is it possible to be proactive and respond smartly, rather than like a poor helpless victim of circumstances?

Changing the window from which I view the boss

The perspective we have always held is that we are 'victims' of bosses who are incompetent, heartless or gutless. We resent bosses who hog the credit, are indecisive or who are inconsiderate and over-demanding. What about doing a 180 degrees shift in this attitude? It involves adopting an outlook, which is far-sighted rather than shortsighted and aims at preparing to win a marathon rather than a 100 metres dash. We are going to be *self-serving and selfish* instead of wasting energies on *self-pity*. We are going to see how to turn the situation to our advantage even in the worst of the situations where the boss:

- is incompetent or doesn't take decisions
- is a ruthless taskmaster
- is never available (to guide or get into details)
- doesn't give credit due to you

Building a better you: It's an opportunity

Len Schlesinger (ex-professor at Harvard Business School) says it's a hard fact of business life: you can't build a better boss. But you can sharpen your skills, advance your career, develop your character—and do it by learning from your boss's foibles and frailties. In other words, the worse you think your boss is, the better the opportunity for you (unbelievable as it may sound in the first instance).

You can't change your boss, but you can build a better you.

1. Learning to take responsibility

My boss is incompetent and has no guts

"Recently I relocated from our factory to the head office in a lateral move as HRD (Human Resources Development) officer. My new boss is sloppy, disorganised and slimy to boot. My very survival is at stake. Here is one of the many instances to illustrate this. One of the projects I was assigned was implementation of the Employee Reward and Recognition Scheme, as well as organising the event. My boss gave me a short-list of 75 awardees (out of an employee strength of 100 employees). When I suggested to my boss that rewarding 75 per cent employees would lose its value, he replied, 'Don't worry about it, the more the merrier.'

"I wanted to inform the awardees in advance, so that the sequencing and timing during the award ceremony would proceed smoothly. Again he disagreed, saying, 'Let there be a surprise element.' Sure enough, at the event there was utter confusion as people milled about the dais. The boss's boss (HR Director) was very displeased. 'There were too many award winners, there was no coordination,' he said. My boss put the blame on my shoulders and said, 'She is responsible for the bungling up.' He didn't even have the decency to provide any support or cover.

"I am now getting the reputation of being ineffectual and inept and I could weep with the despondency of the situation."

—**Shakuntala G., HR Officer*

My boss doesn't take tough decisions

"When it comes to taking a stand or closing a matter my boss gets paralysed—papers just lie on his table, situations and opportunities slip by. He sees himself as very democratic and

* All examples are based on real life situations. Names have been changed to protect identities.

wants to consult the whole of his division so that no one is displeased, inconvenienced, etc. with his decision-making. I feel aggravated as I am suspended in the land of perpetually unresolved issues."

—*Ramesh Sawant, Production Manager*

If your boss is incompetent or indecisive, you actually have a goldmine of an opportunity to develop your own skills in decision-making. Let's say you have burnt your fingers on the first one to two occasions (as in the example above). That's allowed. You can put it into the account of 'life's valuable lessons learnt'. They contribute towards our seasoning and preparing for the future.

But now you have secured a place in a learning school which can help you gauge to what extent your judgements or recommendations are valid. A great idea would be to maintain a diary, where you write your own appraisal and measurement of a situation (what is the decision you would take if you were the boss?) and compare it with what actually happens. This assessment is always possible to make after the event is over and time has unfolded the outcome. You are getting an opportunity to assess your ability to see the future because to make sound judgements is a skill essential for success. This knack does develop with time and experience, though not everyone is able to master it. This situation allows you to fast-forward this education.

You will also have a chance to evaluate to what extent you are willing to stick your neck out, if you could execute your own idea or recommendations. Are you brave enough to push it through with your own signature (metaphorically speaking) at the bottom of the page? The result of the execution will also provide you feedback whether it was an action thought through, with all its implications correctly anticipated. If efforts fall flat, you also discover how to dust your knees and get up. You also learn the value of prudence and caution.

Of course, all this must be preceded by a self-assessment: When you expect a decision from your boss, is he getting the full support he needs from your side? Is back-up data being presented, with relevant research and homework, which will help in arriving at a closure or resolution? Does your proposal clearly document benefits that will accrue to the organisation, or its purpose is primarily to make you look good?

2. Developing a passion for quality

"**My boss is a ruthless taskmaster**—completely to serve her selfish purpose, of course. She drives our team's performance with excruciating deadlines. The worst is that after sitting continuous late nights to complete a project on time, we find that she has actually kept a buffer of five to six days (known only to her). In other words, she lies to us about the actual date of submission of the project (while we work our backs off) just so that she herself is relaxed and ready well in time so as to look good in front of her bosses. This is the third time it has happened, and we are all pretty bugged with her. How can she not trust us with the full project specifications?"

—Raj Mukherjee, Senior Software Engineer

"**My boss is totally inconsiderate**—Here is an instance of his behaviour: On completing a project I was working on a client's site (overseas) till 2 a.m. (my time), which he knew as we were talking on phone right until I went to my hotel to rest. At 6 a.m. (my time) he calls me up (disturbing me from my much required sleep) again to discuss further specifications of the project. I thought that was thoughtless and insensitive."

—Atul Bajaj, Telecom Systems Engineer

The boss is callous and cold-hearted when it comes to driving results and quality; a slave driver who rips you apart when his standards aren't met. He doesn't balk at giving you straight feedback between the eyes and calls a spade a bloody shovel. He really doesn't care if you haven't seen an awake family member for several days; he probably hasn't for several months. You curse and hate his guts as you drive home at night to a cold dinner and a chilly partner.

Here's the paradigm shift: On the one hand, you can view it as a complete nuisance and ego-bruising experience. (Nobody relishes being tightly controlled, or being told that your work is manure.) On the other hand, you can decide to maximise this opportunity to learn to surpass even your own expectations of yourself; constantly measure effectiveness from the perspective of the bottom line; relentlessly drive yourself to reach the highest standards of performance even you didn't know you were capable of.

3. Enlarging the scope of your work

"**My boss is an abdicator** who doesn't like to get his hands dirty with the nuts and bolts. He gives broad and vague directions, which frankly leave me quite confused at times. To compound the problem, he is never available when I want to discuss a plan of action with him. Of course, needless to say, when tasks and goals are accomplished, he is there in the wings to hog all the credit."

—K. Natarajan, Assistant Manager-Marketing

There we go again, the tribe of glory-grabbing bosses is indeed a large one! There is no getting away from them. But now we know that this is a futile and short-term end, and we need to keep our eye on the real goals—the solid work experience. If you are doing all the work—developing the overall plan, implementing it, working late hours, look at the value of the exposure. In your current level, you are actually getting a chance to handle the job description and the role of the next grade! If you had a controlling boss who wouldn't delegate, you would never get the perspective

Getting the perspective of managing a project with a wing-to-wing span is a growth-enabling experience.

of managing a project with a wing-to-wing span with responsibilities at a higher degree than your existing skill-set. Yes, you will feel stretched and lost at times, but heck, it's an enormous opportunity to learn (even if you make mistakes).

4. Putting aside the ego, the 'I'

My boss doesn't give credit due to me

"My boss is a hard taskmaster and drives me crazy with her quest for perfection. Worst is that for all the sweat and toil I drench my tasks with, there is never even a word of praise or encouragement. A recent incident has really shocked and upset me. I prepared a detailed presentation for our overseas visitors, which I gave to my boss on a CD. I later found that she actually erased my name where it said 'prepared by' and replaced it with her own! Is this not unacceptable and unethical behaviour? I have lost all respect as well as motivation to work for her."

—*Laxmi Gopalan, Accounts Manager*

We all have a need for recognition, for acknowledgement of our worth and competence. However, this want sometimes becomes so overwhelming that to fulfill this short-term goal we lose sight of the long-term, which is what smart players focus on—to build solid competencies through the grind of hard work. What is the real bottom line? To add value to my capabilities and skill-set (some say to the bio-data)—by the experience of handling new situations, new territories, developing a proposal, creating a new system, and seeing it through the implementation. What will be my ultimate gain? To explore myself and discover my true proficiencies and talents. If I believe that one day from a caterpillar I will indeed become a butterfly, there is a certain gut-wrenching hard work and sacrifice involved, which means giving up the 'I'.

However, in the desire of wanting to prove too quickly 'I am the greatest' we loose sight of this aim.

If the boss wants all the credit, give it to him.

Such a simple rule, but if you have mastered it, you have mastered your boss! Let him feel great: Allow him to feel he is the author, the creator, the force, and the intelligence behind major initiatives. A very real likelihood is that if you're doing all the work, developing strategies, implementing them, working late nights, those who matter *will* have an understanding of your contribution.

Developing into my full potential requires hard work and sacrifice, and giving up the 'I'.

Raman is an energetic, conscientious and high performing (and intelligent) employee whose boss is thrilled and excited by his performance. During periodic discussions, the boss makes certain suggestions regarding improvement in work areas and possible new projects. There have been instances where Raman has already started implementing them, as he has thought of these ideas on his own. His response? *"Hey, that's a great idea, boss. Let me start work on this right away!"*

Contd.

A week later, he reports back, *"That point you raised at our last meeting—it is all system go. I've put in place step one and there have been very positive reactions from customers."*

The boss, of course, is delighted with Raman's proactive, business-like and upbeat response. So you see, so much gained by resisting the need to say, *"I had already thought of this."*

If you have to disagree because you have a better suggestion, or wish to put up a new initiative, the last thing to use is the direct approach, *"I have an idea, let's do it this way."*

Scott Adams, creator of Dilbert cartoon, says Dilbert would take exactly that approach, because he's an engineer and ignorant of the subtleties of a superior approach! Scott Adams recommends the use of the hypnosis approach—lead the boss through very restrained questions and hints—giving him the impression that it was his idea in the first place!

Here's a thought-provoking example: William Gladstone and Benjamin Disraeli were two powerful statesmen in 19th-century Britain. It is said that when you met Gladstone, you were left with the feeling *he* was the most interesting, charismatic and brilliant person ever. If you spent time with Disraeli, an equally magnetic figure, you felt *you* were the most engaging, captivating and compelling conversationalist.

There is a profound difference. Gladstone sought to impress—with his superior knowledge and articulation skills. Disraeli, on the other hand, made no effort to display (or show off) his abilities. Instead, with his humility and ability to listen and appreciate the other, he made the person feel important. The question is, how do you come across to your boss?

Your boss is your customer—give him what he wants!

I don't like chumming up with my boss

"My boss likes that someone should come and sit with him, chat him up. It gives him a sense of power and position. When I see my colleagues (his other subordinates) chatting up with him, I feel really bugged. Of course, I wouldn't stoop to do it—it's against my value system, plus a colossal waste of company time. If he wants something (information, data, etc.) from me, he can ask for it. I can't read his mind and guess what he wants."

—*Raman Tyagi, Vice President, Logistics*

How do competitive organisations thrive and survive? They woo the person most important to their business—the customer. They talk to him, understand his requirements, and give him what he wants. They aim to delight the customer. They take serious stock of feedback and convince him that he will get value for money and his needs met. The customer feels valued, cared for, understood—and will come again.

How does this apply to your relation with the boss? He is the interface with your organisation—and this relationship—whether pleasant or harmonious, abrasive or competitive, will affect your hour-to-hour and minute-to-minute functioning. It's a choice you exercise—whether to *take* the responsibility for managing it, or *disown* it, leaving it to God, to luck and the boss.

In fact, many of us do take the trouble of 'courting' customers and clients. We go through a lot of effort towards understanding them, tolerating their eccentricities, cultivating the relationship to stay on their right side, and go out of our way to please them by maintaining high standards of performance delivery. Our

The well-prepared subordinate anticipates his boss's requirements!

logical mind understands that this makes business sense, and we are able to do it dispassionately, objectively and unemotionally. Why not maintain the same logic and objectivity with our boss-customer? Why do we allow ourselves to get caught up with our egos here, and get resentful or uptight when the subject comes up of "giving the boss what he wants"?

How do you go about treating the boss like a valued customer? Study the boss-customer carefully. In your interactions, make an effort to understand:

- What are his business delivery needs?
- What is his work style?
- What are his psychological needs?
- What would merely satisfy him? What would delight him?

As Peter Drucker says, "If your boss likes a little reassurance, a little flattery, or if he wants facts and figures or a page of recommendations, then that's what he should get."

Is your boss a 'reader' or 'listener'? Just the way people can be divided into left and right-handers, bosses can be categorised into readers and listeners. If you have a reader for a boss, you wouldn't just go into the office and start talking about a problem or proposal. You would prepare a note and send it in, so that your boss reads it—and *then* you discuss it. Similarly, if your boss were a listener, you would go in and talk about it, and then leave the memo.

If your boss is a stickler for cut-off dates, starting meetings on time, you would have learnt by now that last minute racing-to-meet deadlines doesn't impress him, nor does rushing into a meeting 15 minutes late with breathless excuses. So you pull up your bootstraps and avoid these irritants.

If you find that his preferred mode of communication is SMS, rather than phone, e-mail or face-to-face, wouldn't you use it consistently to contact/appraise him?

So if your boss wants respect and status, then, give it to him. If he wants credit, make him look good in front of your clients, his boss, your colleagues, his colleagues. If he wants you to spend an occasional hour clearing his son's maths problem, it would be a graceful and friendly act. Our ego gets hung up and labels it as apple-polishing.

A person is not all bad or good: Looking beyond black and white.

A person is not all bad: Looking beyond black and white

My boss is a total dud

"My boss is two years younger than me, and the only reason he is sitting on top of me is that he comes from a politically connected family. He comes from a premier management institute, but I am positive he got admission through the quota system (if you know what I mean). I am also pretty sure he has fudged his age.

"He has the brains of a jackass, and doesn't like anyone to question him. I'm not the only one with this view. Others in the organisation also think he's a fool and tell me, 'How can you report to this guy?'

"Of course, he does manage to stay on the right side of his boss by clever political manoeuvring. One of my other colleagues has managed to be his golden boy. He responds to the boss's every requirement with alacrity. If the boss says, hang a balloon, he hangs two—without bothering to find out for what, what pressure of air inside, what colour, etc. I suppose the boss likes it, but that's not my style for sure."

—R. Venugopal, Assistant Vice President (Call Centre)

We often mix up a person's behaviour with the person himself. It is an extreme form of over-generalisation, where, if asked to describe the boss's behaviour, you would say, "He is lousy, rotten, nasty, spiteful, a political manoeuvrer, and self-serving." You paint in your mind an entirely negative picture of the person, and *everything* about him grates, and becomes unacceptable—from his walk to work style. (I once knew a subordinate who found even her boss's laugh objectionable.) Feelings of hostility increase, and it becomes impossible to view the boss in a more objective manner.

Is this rational or distorted thinking? Let us use logic. Can you really have a total write-off who has been selected by a system in a position of responsibility? He must be delivering some goods (if his boss thinks well of him); and as per the above cribber's own admission, he has a constructive working relationship with the other subordinate (golden boy).

The first step is to realise that your perception has got locked in a single-dimension view (which you would love to believe is the universal reality, but isn't the case). The next step is to write on a sheet of paper a list of negative terms to describe his behaviour (*see* Table 1). On the same sheet, force yourself to write some positive aspects of his behaviour.

Finally, write down some aspects that are neutral—some of the things he says or does that are neither good nor bad. With this exercise you are forcing yourself to keep in mind a more complete, less one-sided and more precise view of him.

Table 1

Describing the boss's behaviour in negative terms	*Describing the boss's behaviour in positive terms*	*Describing the boss's behaviour in neutral terms*
1. Lousy	1. Forthright, speaks his mind out.	1. Doesn't drink or smoke.
2. Rotten	2. Very social and well networked within the organisation.	2. Sings well.
3. Nasty	3. Extremely articulate and excellent in presentation skills.	3. Is the father of 10-year old twins.
4. Spiteful	4. Helpful and considerate towards other people.	4. Is an active member of the Ramakrishna Mission.
5. A political manoeuvrer	5. Aggressive and determined when it comes to pushing for resources.	5. Enjoys tennis.
6. Self-serving	6. Acts in his self-interests (very much like me)	

Consciously train yourself to associate his reference with a more neutral and objective picture of him: A person who is small and thinly built, with salt and pepper hair, enjoys tennis, who is fair sometimes and unfair at times, who is both reasonable and unreasonable. You will be able to reduce the unhappiness, irritation and anger you feel towards him every time you have to interact with him or think of him. The idea is to de-emphasise his bad traits and acquire a more impartial, detached, clear and open-minded view of him.

3

Types of Bosses and How to Deal with Them

In the last chapter our emphasis was on the subordinate's attitude—how that plays a key role in making or breaking your career. We now move to the next step of analysing different types of bosses so that our responses to them can be further customised and fine-tuned!

As we set out to study the flora and fauna of the boss's world, luckily there is no dearth of variety: The fumbler and bumbler, ruthless and manipulative, credit grabber and slave driver. On the other hand, they can be intelligent and focused with a clear vision, open-minded and trustworthy, large hearted, courageous and dynamic go-getters.

For our convenience, we will sort bosses into these four types, using a simple matrix:

- The bully or toxic boss
- The lost-in-the-fog boss
- The agreeable-but-undemanding boss
- The growth enabler or ideal boss

Our model is based on two facets of boss's qualities. The first is **competence**—the ability to:

- contribute to the bottom line by meeting targets;
- drive change by intelligent foresight, strategy and meticulous implementation;
- handle detractors through political savvy.

The second is **leadership**—which includes:

- concern for people;
- ability to carry and motivate employees;
- capacity to see their potential even when they have not;
- risk taking to delegate authority and responsibility.

Table 2

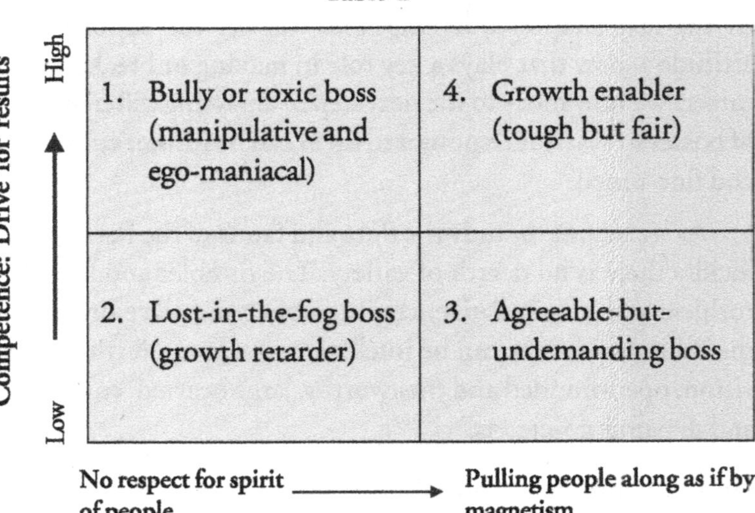

1. Bully or toxic boss (manipulative and ego-maniacal)	4. Growth enabler (tough but fair)
2. Lost-in-the-fog boss (growth retarder)	3. Agreeable-but-undemanding boss

Leadership:
- **Carries people with him**
- **Believes in their potential and brings out their best**

I. The worst is the bully or the toxic boss

1. "My boss leaves me totally drained and stressed out. Whenever things go the slightest bit wrong, he yells and belittles us (his team), crossing boundaries of self-dignity, at times even in front of my juniors.

"The confusing part is that he doesn't make it clear in the first place what he wants. He gives vague and unclear directions, leaving it to us to figure out through guesswork and 'mind-reading' what he expects. In addition, he keeps so busy, that he is unavailable to provide clarifications.

"When we present our work to him, he tears and rips it apart in a scathing and humiliating manner, as it is not what he had visualised. This kind of behaviour leaves me depressed and devalued."

—Atul Shukla, Assistant Vice President, Credit Cards

2. "My boss and I seemed to have rubbed each other the wrong way right from the start. My job is to recruit manpower in large members. Even though I work at breakneck pace to fill in routine organisational requirements, he is constantly needling me with questions like, 'What value-add are you bringing to your role?' He also tries to push me with unrealistic expectations, giving me assignments requiring skill sets I don't have (I have a total of two years' experience after my MBA). Recently he wanted me to design a database of resumes in Oracle and Access. When I told him I would need time to learn and implement it, he used the foulest language to indicate his impatience and scorn.

"I feel I am treated like a second-class citizen and that my very value as a human being is being negated."

—Puneet Sharma, Assistant HR Manager

These are fine examples of models of bully bosses—unbalanced, ego-maniacal and brutal. They react with anger and

The bully or toxic boss.

fierceness when wishes are not complied with, and assert control by frightening employees and putting them down. Their tempers flare up so suddenly that they seem to go out of control. There is little regard for the dignity or sensitivity of juniors.

Often they see themselves as all-powerful dictators, and are capable of punishing and destroying anyone who gets in their way or questions their authority. They have no qualms about finding a scapegoat when things go wrong. They can also be exploitative, handing down assignments with excruciating and unreasonable deadlines when it suits them. There is a blatant lack of concern for your life—"Your personal problems are not my concern", and imply a master-servant status where they can do or say anything they please.

Very clearly, the only reason they push subordinates is that they themselves can climb further and further up the organisational ladder.

Some characteristic behaviours could include:

- screaming profanities in public or putting the subordinate down with comments like, "I can't believe you made that mistake again";
- refusing to share critical information regarding total project perspective, or even correct deadlines;
- giving vague or conflicting instructions, which change according to their whims and fancies;
- thrashing the subordinate at every opportunity—often over small things like the quality of a memo written, "Didn't they teach you English paragraph-writing in school?"
- attempting to micromanage every situation, asking for endless details, questioning every decision made.

It can cause damage

First of all, be assured that it is a more common problem than you thought. According to a recent study, four out of five employees will deal with it at some point during their careers. Secondly, victims of brutal bosses can end up feeling so lost, isolated, shaky and depressed that it erodes self-esteem and can leave a person feeling inadequate with strong feelings of self-blame. Studies have shown this phenomenon resulting into serious health problems like sleep disorders, high blood pressure, ulcers and irritable colon.

Why do such bosses survive and thrive? Often because they deliver the goods for their bosses, who are either oblivious or turn a blind eye. Indeed they have developed the ability and reputation of meeting difficult targets, pushing through impossible ventures, bringing home victories for the company. They are highly competent and intelligent, and management sees them as having that 'edge'. Of course, this is a narrow and limited view, as when people are left de-energised and de-motivated, the results will most likely be short-lived.

Dealing with the bully boss

Chapter nine ('Bosses who Harass and Terrorise') covers in detail how to deal with this kind of person. However, some simple strategies are:

- build your own credibility and network within the organisation by being helpful to internal customers/other departmental heads;
- while it is essential you should talk out your problem with a person you trust; don't make it a habit to launch into a tirade of your grievances and gripes at every opportunity with anybody who is willing to give you a supportive ear or shoulder (specially within the organisation);
- seek help from the Human Resources Department.

II. Lost-in-the-fog boss

"My boss maintains such a low profile that we might as well be a ghost ship in the fog. His unspoken motto is 'don't row the boat—don't rock the boat'. He avoids taking any risky decisions, and quite strictly follows a rule of 'I'm not here to light fuses', and sets great store in following, guarding and maintaining the existing systems and practices. When I try to take the initiative to bring improvements, he gets quite agitated, and does everything possible to obstruct it. He rarely shares with his juniors his thoughts (if any) on future plans, long-term goals of our section.

"To make matters worse, when other section heads push or pummel him, he just takes it lying down, although he is fuming inwardly I know." —*Vikas Lobo, Assistant Manager, MIS*

The lost-in-the-fog or ostrich boss dislikes change and takes refuge in being conservative and cautious.

The growth-retarding or clueless boss is best suitable (for a limited period of time) to learn the ropes of the existing systems and procedures from; and at worst is a bottleneck or roadblock to further growth, new ideas and approaches. Not the sharpest crayon in the box, he has limited capabilities for problem solving, for anticipating and reacting to change, indeed, for developing any vision or strategy, he takes refuge in being conservative and cautious.

He avoids limelight, confrontation or conflict. He rarely pushes back when peers' demands become aggressive, finding some short-term solution to deal with the dissatisfaction arising, and has learnt the art of surviving. Subordinates who are more capable than him also threaten him.

Dealing with the lost-in-the-fog boss

This person has a high need for safety and security, and strives to create an environment for himself where there is order, stability and predictability.

- It might seem that the sole purpose of these idiot bosses is to agitate and annoy their employees. However, it's not a good idea to confront, or to make it known in any indirect way that you feel exasperated with this ostrich boss. Remember, they have as much power over our moods as we allow them to have.
- Nor is it a good scheme to 'arrange' for him to be embarrassed at a meeting so that you can look good in front of your seniors (tempting though it may be).

  One subordinate who worked in a garments export factory found to her dismay that her boss was not concerned even when she brought to his notice that production quotas were not being met, and they were falling behind deadlines. She had also experienced unprecedented last-minute panic the previous season as a result of his slack control of time-lines. Without putting her boss down, she exerted pressure by calling for a meeting with his peers, tactfully suggesting that production be speeded up through working overtime, rescheduling of other lines, etc. She was able to meet her targets despite her boss, and more importantly, without making him look foolish.
- It's an opportunity to take on more responsibilities (very slowly). If you focus on your work, and not worry about office politics, you can be quite productive.
- Phrase your suggestions as questions, and make your boss think your ideas are his: "Do you think if we set up an online customer feedback system, we might get useful data about customer responsiveness for the new product?"

- Instead of asking open-ended questions, present limited options and one clear recommendation. If the boss is vague, nudge him gently towards specifics.
- Document your work as evidence of your capabilities. One way of doing this is to update your boss formally (on e-mail or on paper) how your projects/assignments are going, including in it a short paragraph on your suggestion.
- Talk to the Human Resources Department and apply for another job within the company.
- Plan your exit (say within a time-frame of the next one year). This can make a huge difference in the way you view your 'term' in your job.

III. Agreeable-but-undemanding boss

"I have such a comfortable job; an outsider would think I'm crazy to be cribbing. My boss likes to run her department like a big happy family. She is like a mother figure—she rarely pulls up anyone, or takes a tough or harsh decision. She also likes to have a coterie of favourites around her—people whom over the years she has developed comfort levels with.

On the flip side, because of her dislike for hard stands, she tries to please everyone. One fall-out (for example) is that the unionised staff, which reports to me, has free access to her. Her message to them is 'My doors are always open'. Their often (ridiculous) demands are accommodated by her. Unfortunately, in a very subtle way, this is not only undermining my authority, but I am finding it increasingly difficult to maintain standards of discipline and work performance."

—K. Natarajan, Senior Manager, Administration

To their credit, these friendly bosses do create a comfortable team climate with their warm and caring style. They also tend to give young members a chance to develop and grow. However, their need to be liked and loved is higher than their need to be

The agreeable-but-undemanding boss runs his department like a big, happy family.

respected. Hence they rarely push or confront people to deliver beyond their limits, as they don't want to make people angry, though they themselves get hurt easily.

They may also tend to take on too seriously the role of a 'parent' and in the process overdo both—nurturing and control. For instance, in the event of an employee falling ill, they would show great concern, recommending doctors, medicines, and pushing them to go home and rest. On the other hand, they strongly disapprove if others' actions don't match their prescribed norms, and can exert pressure with their demands of conformity.

Dealing with the agreeable boss

Coping with the agreeable boss is of course the easiest of the four boss types. The problem is that given their high need for approval, deliverables and work excellence get a lower priority. Real and hard feedback is avoided; with the result that rigorous learning and growth opportunity take a backseat, which won't get you very far.

- While you demonstrate suitable regard to your boss, watch out for submissive or fawning behaviour. This will 'hook' the parent in them and will tend to treat you more like a kid than a subordinate. Their expectations of unquestioned obedience will escalate, which will become difficult to handle later.
- Maintain a very invisible boundary of formal respect, and don't get too familiar. In moments of chumminess, it is very easy and tempting to let your guard slip, and confide your deepest desires, dreams, secrets and weaknesses. At that time it may feel intoxicatingly free, but this never works at work. Such openness exposes vulnerabilities which will come back to haunt you later.
- Even in the middle of a heated discussion (certainly there will be conflict even with this buddy-boss) keep your cool.

IV. The growth enabler or ideal boss

This happens to a lucky few—a boss who is dynamic and high-powered, who has vision, wisdom and business acumen. He has the courage to think big, and the perseverance to implement his vision and plans. He is apolitical, and has the guts to stick to a stand when others are buck-passing or sitting on the fence. He has the large heartedness to take risks, and willingly delegates authority to subordinates believing in their potential and growth.

He has no qualms about sharing the spotlight, readily giving credit where it's due. He enjoys a reputation of being caring, fair and trustworthy. Good at reading people's character and skill set, he is sensitive to personal issues. His integrity is above question,

The growth enabler or ideal boss.

and is disciplined about and committed to work standards.

Because he is so extremely results-driven, to those subordinates who can't or won't run at his tempo, he can appear ruthless in demanding performance. He has no patience for slackers or laggards, and can take the unemotional decision of 'letting go' if required for the sake of his bottom line. Such bosses are always focused and in control.

But to those who show horsepower, he is willing to be their mentor and provide limitless opportunities to grow and move up.

Dealing with the growth enabler

- Because of their relentless drive for high standards of performance, you better make sure you pace the growth enabler in his demands of outstanding results. There are no shortcuts here for working your tail off!
- Take the initiative and demonstrate enthusiasm. If there are extra projects you can take outside your regular work duties, which are some of your boss's dream projects, do them, and importantly, do them cheerfully.
- Go through details, facts and figures, making sure they are error-free.
- Demonstrate your support and loyalty by both—consistently delivering quality tasks as well as being his champion. At all times, hold up a positive and winning image of your boss in the organisation.

Bosses don't always fit into neat categories

The descriptions of the four types of bosses here are of an extreme type, and in real life, bosses don't fit in so tidily! Most of us (thankfully) are able to see some redeeming qualities in our bosses.

"Even though she can be a real pain, I respect her. She speaks her mind. She gets things done. I just wish she wouldn't sit on my head and micromanage things. But I know it's not intentional."

"I really appreciate the clarity with which he states his expectations and goals. That makes a real pleasure to work with him. But at times when he goes berserk in his anxiety..."

"He gives us a broad canvas to work on, and I like to take my own initiative. But how I wish he would pick up the phone and just speak to his seniors when things get stuck, but he just washes his hands off messy problems. He's an abdicator of painful issues..."

"I've learnt a lot of sales from him. If only he would delegate more."

In the chapters that follow, we are going to look at how to communicate with the boss on tricky issues, to give feedback in a frank and respectful manner, how to get the boss's attention, and how to speak in a situation that makes us nervous and anxious.

Understanding My Boss's Personality and Mine

While it was helpful to identify four broad styles and patterns of boss's behaviour in the last chapter (and learn how to deal with them), we need to guard against putting people in boxes! It has the danger of blinding us to some of their more positive or neutral personality characteristics. And the fact remains we still need to accept them as human beings and work with them. Let us look towards deepening our understanding of the boss's personality and mine.

Using a scientific framework

One framework of grasping and analysing the Personality Type is the Myers Briggs Type Indicator (MBTI)® instrument. It was developed as far back as 1930s on the basis of Swiss psychologist Carl Jung's work of more than 80 years ago. Jung suggested that human behaviour was not random but in fact predictable and therefore classifiable. A mother-daughter team, Katherine Briggs and Isabel Briggs Myers, designed a psychological instrument that explains in scientifically rigorous and reliable terms the differences in personalities. Today the MBTI is one of the most widely used frameworks for understanding human behaviour across the world.

Even if you have not had the opportunity to take the MBTI test, the following descriptions of the different personality types will help you in understanding your own type, and more importantly, your boss's. One of the great advantages of type classification is that it is judgement-free. There are no good or bad 'types' and it aims to create an understanding of the characteristics of people (bosses)—whether it is talking too much or not talking enough, obsessing about nitty-gritty or glossing over details, working from a tightly structured schedule or operating in a 'free-flow' manner. It helps us move away from name-calling in a negative, 'one-up' or evaluative way resulting in distance and distrust to more healthy and neutral interpretations.

The MBTI describes four pairs of dimensions (described below), which are present to some degree in all people. As you go through the two extreme (or opposite) descriptions of each of the four dimensions, try to identify which fits you better. Remember that no one will fit neatly in either pair as in real life we are a mixture of both sides. However, each individual does have one innate preference, however slight, over the other. This preference is shown and practised by an individual in a fairly consistent way over his entire lifetime, and developed very early in life.

1. The expressive vs the reserved boss

The first preference described in the two columns below has to do with people who get their personal energy from the outer world of people, things and action (Extraversion); or from the inner world of thoughts, ideas and concepts (Introversion).

Table 3

Extraverts 'E'	*Introverts 'I'*
Need to verbalise; tend to talk to express themselves, to clarify their thoughts, to understand things.	Need to reflect. They first 'process' thoughts inside their heads, then present them to the outside world; may leave some thoughts unshared.
In meetings tend to take up a lot of 'air time', i.e. speak at length.	In meetings, may be attentive listeners, but say a few chosen words.
Think on their feet, and act and respond quickly.	Could respond with, "Let me think and get back to you."
Prefer oral communication. Their basic approach is, "Let's talk things over."	Prefer written communication.
Gain energy by interacting.	Feel drained out by interacting with people: need time to be alone; may like to work with the office door closed.
May have broad (several) interests; tend to be generalists; willing to act on limited or 'superficial' information.	May have deep but few interests; tend to be specialists; like to go in-depth in relevant work subject.
Are approachable and relate easily with friends, co-workers and strangers; have relationships with many people.	Are uncomfortable with small talk; are unenthusiastic in making social contact for the sake of it; have limited but deep relationships.
Come across as easily accessible and easy to know.	Can come across as reseved, reflective or aloof.
Share their feelings, thoughts and opinions freely.	Wait to be asked before they share.

What is your assessment of:

a) Your type? 'I' or 'E' ________

b) Your boss's type? 'I' or 'E' ________

The 'E' talks to express himself and gains energy by interacting.

Can you identity your type—whether 'E' or 'I'? Can you identify your boss's type? It is possible that if you have ticked five items on the left column, you have ticked two or four items from 'I' column also. Thus you may see parts of your personality in *both* the columns, but one column will describe more closely your *basic* or *natural* preference.

Many times we behave in certain ways because the situation demands it (e.g. an experienced 'I' salesman would (need to) behave like an 'E' with his customers.) Hence, think deeply before selecting the column that describes the real you and your boss—the latter, of course, you would guess from the observed traits and characteristics.

If you and your boss are of opposite personality types, chances of conflict and misunderstanding can increase!

Some suggestions to deal with an 'I' boss

- Put agenda/ thoughts in writing before a meeting and send it to him. This helps, as an 'I' likes to have time to mull over an idea before he responds to it.
- At discussion time, focus on the topic. Don't expect to engage in small talk.
- The 'I' does not take kindly to unexpected and unscheduled interruptions. Hence if you want time for discussion, it is best to fix in advance, where the agenda for the meeting is also made clear.
- The 'I' sometimes tends to speak slowly, with pauses in conversations. At such times, don't rush in to fill in those pauses with your own worldviews.
- Allow the 'I' boss time alone after long interactive sessions. If, after a conference, he isn't too keen to join a beer or bowling session, it doesn't mean he's snooty or uppity—he just needs his 'alone' time to unwind.
- Don't be disheartened if praise is not forthcoming. Instead make it a point to ask for feedback occasionally (how a project was handled, a presentation made, etc.) and be prepared for negative feedback.

  Acknowledge it with "Thanks for the feedback, it was really useful".
- The 'I' feels uncomfortable with too much praise. (He feels it is phony, superficial and unnecessary). So if you are stroking your boss, don't overdo it!

Some suggestions to deal with an 'E' boss

- The 'E' fills space around him with words, and words. One reason is that he is clarifying his own thoughts as he speaks. These statements may not be his final verdict. Hence, before you start action on some of the assertions, recheck with the boss on his priorities (or wait until he mentions it again!).
- The 'E' needs you to be a good and patient listener. Often he does

The 'I' feels drained out by interacting with people and needs to 're-charge' himself by being alone.

not need more than occasional nodding, smiling, frowning, and continued attention. If you are the kind who doesn't speak much, you will also have to learn to 'make' your own leg-room and tell your side of the story.

- Have a list of things (in your mind or on paper) you want to cover in your meeting, and make sure you wrap them up. Otherwise The 'E' can 'take over' the conversation, and the track can get diverted to various other topics and sub-topics.
- The 'E' sets great store on presentation skills, being active and articulate in meetings and group discussions. Hence it's a good idea to polish up these abilities.

II. The 'big picture' (don't-bother-me-with-details) vs the 'are-we-meeting-tomorrow's-numbers' boss

The second preference described below is whether people experience the world through their five senses, paying attention to facts and present realities—Sensing 'S'; or whether they are more interested in the future or some timeless principle—iNtuition 'N'.

Table 4

Sensors 'S'	iNtuitives 'N'
Rely on their five senses as means of gathering information—they pay attention to only things they can see, hear, touch, taste or smell.	As information is gathered through the five senses they translate it through intuition, looking for meanings, links and possibilities.
Think in factual, step-by-step manner, e.g. on being shown a *gulmohar* flower and asked, "What do you see?" the response will be literal "A red flower, large petals, no fragrance."	Think imaginatively, randomly, in leaps and bounds. The reply to the same question may be, "It reminds me of my childhood home in Ranchi; we had a tree in front of our house."
Prefer to focus on concrete facts, details and specifics than ideas and theories (see the trees).	Look for the overall picture, future possibilities, relationship with a broader conceptual framework (see the forest).
Like to give (and receive) literal and specific information (e.g. instructions might be, "Take the first left turn, then you will see a public school signboard, 500 yards ahead is a red iron gate. Our	Tend to give general answers; get bored by "unnecessary" details. (Instructions might be given as, "It's next to the park. You'll find it easily.")

Contd.

building is in the second block from right.")	
Get frustrated when people don't give clear feedback/instructions.	Feel pushed /irritated when required to go into specifics; tend to give general answers/ instructions: "We'll need to rework this"; "These are broadly our objectives—we'll work out the details later."
Like to rely on their own experience/ proven ways to solve problems.	Get excited by novel, innovative (perhaps untried) ideas.
Like to work on tasks/ projects with tangible end results; prefer goals that are simple and attainable; fancy goals to them are ridiculous.	Goals need to be inspirational, challenging, "to dream the impossible dream".
Hate to see people making things more complicated than they are.	Enjoy complexity, theoretical frameworks.
Are sensible, practical, and down to earth.	Are imaginative, innovative, head in clouds, full of future possibilities.

What is your assessment of:

a) Your type? N or S ....

b) Your boss's type? N or S ....

Some suggestions to deal with an 'N' boss

- If you hear suggestions, ideas that sound far-fetched, don't be too quick to dismiss them. Hear them out –there may be something in them, even though they may seem to you a flight of wild goose taking off into never-never land. Show interest, ask questions.

The 'S' prefers to focus on concrete facts, details and specifies.
The 'N' looks for meanings and possibilities.

- When discussing the solution to a current problem, mention how it will affect the future. Link it, if possible, to a new and exciting idea.
- The 'N' tends to reject simple solutions as he prefers complexity and likes to view things within a larger framework of theoretical concepts. Hence, when presenting a solution, first generate various alternatives and put them on the table.
- If you are presenting many facts, arrange them in sub-categories, which in turn have some relationship. Remember the 'N' likes meaningful patterns, and is irritated with a lot of data.
- When asking for feedback, avoid generalities like, "What do you think of the report?" Instead make it specific, "Can you give me feedback on sections X and Y of the report?"

- Once his idea has been rolled out, the 'N' is impatient with routine and step-by-step implementation. If as a subordinate you can fill this gap (it is easier if you are an 'S') and take care of all the details and nitty-gritties of execution, you can be an indispensable right hand, whom the boss will learn to lean on.

Some suggestions to deal with an 'S' boss

- If you are presenting a new project or solution, explain it briefly and simply.
- If possible, find an example (from the past or from the environment or industry) similar to what you are proposing, as evidence that your idea works.
- Also think through practical outcomes and applications of your concept or idea, along with specific and concrete steps of implementation, especially in the first stages.
- Suggest a dry run or a test period for a fixed time for putting through a proposed change.
- 'S' prefers to hear facts in a sequential manner ("I suggest we do a test market survey for our proposed product. This entails three steps: first is....; second is...; third is...")
- Check your work for errors in calculations, facts, etc. which the 'N' is prone to overlook in favour of the large picture (or sheer inspiration!). This is the first thing an 'S' will notice.
- Do meet the 'S' boss's requirements of immediate task completion, numbers, and monthly targets!

III. The tough-minded vs the friendly boss

The third trait refers to how people make decisions based on objective, non-personal assessment by Thinking 'T', or on the basis of subjective personal values by Feeling 'F'.

When dealing with an 'F' boss

- Keep track, if you are alienating people whilst aggressively pressing a goal or an issue.
- In your proposal, the 'F' is sure to raise points regarding people's

The Thinker 'T' takes decisions in a rational, logical and impartial manner.

views, i.e. how people will feel, how they will get affected. Work out answers in advance.

- The 'F' boss has difficulty in giving negative/ unpleasant criticism, and lack of any does not mean that none exists. You will need to tactfully dig out the feedback and the boss's real views.
- At a discussion, before getting on to bass tracks, do spend a few minutes on, "Hello, how's the old backache?"
- Genuinely express appreciation (occasionally) for the support, time and advice you are getting from your boss!

Table 5

Thinkers 'T'	*Feelers 'F'*
Take a decision in a rational, logical, impartial manner based on what they believe to be fair and correct by predefined rules of behaviour.	Take a decision on the individual case in a subjective manner, based on what they believe to be right within their own value system.
Impersonalise—think objectively from outside the situation.	Personalise, i.e. put themselves into the shoes of the other to ask, "How would I feel if this were done to me?"
Enjoys a good 'healthy' argument; sometimes argue to prove a point.	Dislike and avoid conflicts and differences of opinion; to them opposing views create tension.
Give more importance to reaching a logical goal than taking care of people's feelings, or ensuring that all opinions are heard.	Take time to listen to employee's concerns, or resolve an issue that is bothering someone.
When it comes to unpleasant interactions (like reprimanding an employee, dealing with a conflict), they will prefer to complete it quickly and have it out of the way (though they won't relish it).	Avoid unpleasant interactions; value harmony at all costs.
Deal with discord by discussing it out and planning in advance (like playing chess).	Get emotionally involved and may blame themselves for the conflict.
Minimise emotional reactions; allergic to 'losing control'.	May react physically, e.g. crying, yelling, sweating; could loose control and say things they will later regret.

What is your assessment of :

a. Your type? : F or T ....

b. Your boss's type? : F or T ....

The Feeler 'F' takes a decision in a subjective manner, based on what is believed to be right within own value system.

When dealing with a 'T' boss

- Get to the point quickly without getting into much of, "Hello, how are things going?"
- Before the conversation, think about what you want to present and get accepted. If there are issues, which you 'feel' are right, identify objective reasons to support your recommendations.
- When the 'T' boss disagrees or rejects a proposal, don't treat it as a personal rebuff. Taking it personally can result in bruised feelings, brooding, and loss of productivity. You have two choices—drop it; or over a second round, try to convince the boss through more facts, homework, etc.

- Similarly, if the 'T' boss asks for clarification or further data, don't personalise the situation. Focus on the facts rather than your own feelings of irritation or being upset.
- Don't expect too much praise or appreciation for your contribution from a 'T' boss.
- Keep in mind that the 'T' is uncomfortable with open display of emotions like crying, hugging and showing warmth.

IV. The well-organised-and-structured vs the free-flowing and 'let's-wait-and-see' boss

The last trait refers to how people prefer to run their lives. Those preferring Judging 'J', like a lifestyle that is prearranged and organised, orderly and established. Those preferring Perceiving 'P', want things to be spontaneous and unstructured, often not closing a decision until the last moment. In this area, differences in working style with your boss can really drive you up the wall.

Ways of dealing with the 'P' boss

One difficulty with 'P' is that he rarely takes a stand. The reason is that he is so open-minded that he sees all the shades of grey and ever-changing possibilities in a situation, as opposed to sticking with one alternative and taking action.

He also resists closing a decision because he wants to evaluate further (and better) options he feels are waiting just 'around the corner'. It is quite possible that in the middle of a situation he will consider another alternative and in the process lose sight of the end result.

However, because of these traits, the 'P' is able to bring to the table innovative and better quality solutions, provided he learns to 'force' himself to close decisions.

Table 6

Judgers 'J'	*Perceivers 'P'*
Prefer to work with an organised and preplanned schedule, which they like to adhere to (even building in time to relax!)	Are more flexible, adaptable; like to go with the flow, take things as they come; even if they start with a list, they need not necessarily follow it.
Prefer things to be neat, orderly and organised; have a 'place for everything and everything in its place'.	While having a preference for neatness, they do not set a high priority on it
Like to close a decision quickly–on the basis of available data.	Prefer to wait for more information so that more alternatives are generated. Hence, they are willing to keep decisions 'open' for as long as possible.
Don't like last-minute changes and surprises; like things settled.	Don't like to be pinned down about most things, preferring to keep options open.
Like to finalise matters/tasks and get them out of the way.	In the process of completing a task, can get distracted into attending to other, perhaps unrelated activities, leaving the original work incomplete.
Are particular about deadlines and prefer to complete tasks ahead of time.	May meet deadlines, but with a last minute rush, which leaves everyone 'frazzled'.
Motto is 'work before play'.	Motto is 'play before work'.
View time as finite units of commodity that have to be utilised 'now'.	View time as an expandable, elastic commodity ("I can always find time later.")

What is your assessment of

a. Your type? : P or J .....

b. Your boss' type? : P or J.....

The Perceiver 'P', "There are so many possibilities and solutions... Let's wait for some more time before deciding..."

So, with a 'P' boss, the challenge lies in resolution and moving on. Here are some suggestions:

- If he brings up more options/ demands for changes/ change of direction, acknowledge it tactfully (putting aside your irritation) and move towards conclusion, saying, "Thanks for this perspective, it wouldn't have occurred to me. I will incorporate it in the new plan. Can we work on step one?"
- When you leave your proposal, stitch in a time-line of when you want a discussion. "I've prepared a document on the revised accounting system. Can you look at it and give me your views by Thursday?"
- Request for periodic meetings where you review and update your boss.

The Judger 'J' likes to close a decision quickly, on the basis of available data.

- Don't offer the 'P' boss new ideas once a solution has been arrived at.

Dealing with a 'J' boss

The 'J' likes to close matters and move on. His need for judgement, to settle the matter, to control the environment, to stay on schedule is so great that it may seem the decision has been taken before considering the full range of options, (even) before consulting you. It may come across as too fast, presumptuous and autocratic.

The 'J' sees the world as black and white, right and wrong and has difficulty in accepting opposing points of view.

When dealing with a 'J' boss

- If a decision has been taken (the basis of which you cannot figure out), put aside your annoyance and ask for details or clarification. "Could I request you to share with me your basis for this approach?"
- The 'J' dislikes having his diary interrupted. If 3.00-4.00 p.m. is set aside for e-mails, he will not take kindly to being requested for an emergency meeting at this time. Similarly, if a meeting is scheduled, he expects the timings and agenda to be followed. It is best to avoid springing surprises on him.
- The 'J's' statements can give the impression that things are decided and foreclosed; he is sure he is right, and there is no room for negotiation. (Some call him opinionated and 'know-it all'.) This can cause others to shrink back and 'agree along'. However, the 'J' is not necessarily right. If you have suggestions or opinions backed by data and facts, you must bring them up.
- Quick decisions are not necessarily the best. They may serve an immediate bottom-line requirement, but for long-term solutions, the more people are involved, the longer it may take, but higher the commitment and quality of decision. So, you can press for additional information towards the goal of higher quality.

Your boss's (and your) four-letter combination

After reading the description of the above dimensions, you should be able to choose one from each of the four pairs of preferences.

Table 7

	My preferences	*My boss's preferences*
Extraversion (E) or Introversion (I)		
Sensing (S) or iNtuition (N)		
Thinking (T) or Feeling (F)		
Judging (J) or Perceiving (P)		

Each preference interacts with others to form 16 different combinations, which means there are 16 different types of personalities, e.g. ISTJ, INFP, ENFP, ENTJ, etc. (However each individual is still unique, e.g. if you have met two ESTJs, with some experience, you would be able to see similarities, but each would be different expressions of the same type).

Let's say you have identified your boss to be an ISTJ (which is one of the most frequently occurring types in senior management). This would help in understanding his personality: He probably likes time alone to think things over ('I'), and may prefer to look over a proposal before discussing it. He is practical and interested in immediate details ('S') and concrete data, preferring to work with proven or established ideas/systems, rather than future possibilities, challenges and new ideas ('N'). When he makes decisions, he is more concerned about the bottom line of facts and figures ('T') than how it will affect him or others ('F'). Using judging means, he likes things planned out ('J'), and tends to be organised and follows a time-table than playing it by the ear or leaving things to the last moment ('P').

With just these four letters, you can have a lot of information about yourself and your boss.

Learning to accept the boss's personality

So, instead of getting into a spiral of thinking:

"I wish he would say what is in his mind instead of me having to second guess what is behind that aloof expression."

"No one seems to bother about the big picture. I'm fed up of running after next month's targets without understanding the strategy."

"I wish he would be less of a cold-blooded rob-cop and more human."

"I wish he would take a decision and stick to it."

The MBTI teaches us to understand, be aware of and appreciate (even value) where the boss is coming from.

5

Building Bridges of Communication with the Boss

Suppose you went to a dentist who said, "Your tooth needs a root canal treatment, but we'll do it without anaesthesia, as I am out of supplies today." You would be out faster than he could say, 'P.T. Usha'. Communication with the boss is as important as an anaesthesia is in tooth extraction, or any surgery! Without it, your work life is going to be unbearable—in addition to the pain, you will have to contend with tension, misunderstanding and friction.

Keep in mind boss's different communication styles

We have already seen in the earlier pages that all individuals have their own preferences and traits in how they approach and do things. Acting in response to them does not mean ingratiating yourself or 'changing colours like a chameleon to suit the boss', as one employee dismissed it indignantly.

- Does he like to get into details, or is he a 'broad brush-strokes' person?

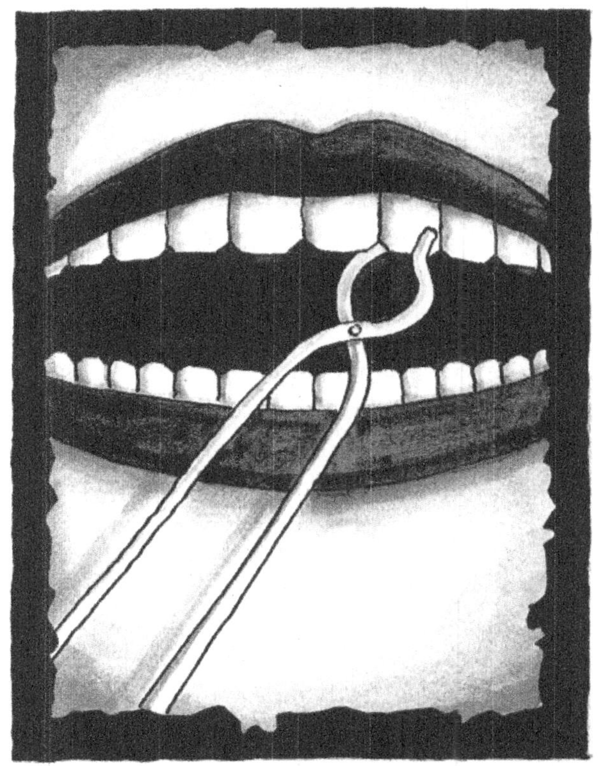

Communication with the boss is as important as an anaesthesia is in tooth extraction.

- In meetings does he strictly stick to the agenda, or is he all over the map and likes a free-flowing discussion?
- Does he prefer to have something in writing before a discussion or after a discussion?
- Does he like you to seek his advice and counsel, or does he prefer you to take independent decisions?
- When his door is closed, does he dislike to be disturbed, or you can knock and still walk in?
- Does he hate small talk? Then be polite and quickly come to the point.
- If he is a quiet person, don't assume silence means agreement. Try asking him what he is thinking!

- In a presentation, what is he more impressed with—content or window-dressing?

Rigidity and blockage can come from us

A subordinate by his very role is expected to listen. He is required to receive instructions and directions; understand the boss's point of view; obtain facts and details; listen to feedback about his work. However, listening is not as easy and automatic as it sounds!

What are the barriers that come in the way of listening? The main interference is a static disturbance in the conversation in the form of a parallel 'chatter' that is going on inside our heads. Even as we are outwardly talking with the boss, there is an inward running commentary the mind engages in. Do you recognise any of it?

- "What's the point of trying? He'll never agree!" or
- "I hope I don't make a fool of myself...maybe I shouldn't open my mouth," or
- "I've made such a fantastic point, I'm sure he'll be impressed by my knowledge," or
- "What does he know about this subject? But doesn't he love to hear his own voice..."

Where do these come from?

- Our own assumptions and biases, which cause us to jump to conclusions.
- Our own past experiences or even hearsay.
- A belief that our views are better and more superior.

This attachment to our view causes us to be closed to the other's point, resulting in rigidity and blockage in communication. When the mind is listening to this chatter, two problems are created: One, we miss out on important information/instructions, and two, we are liable to misinterpret what the boss is saying.

It's important to be alert to this internal mind chatter, which is nothing but a manifestation of our prejudices and our own rigidity.

Keeping an open mind

Even whilst raising our point, it's extremely important to be open to the fact that the other person may have a perspective, equally valid, from his point of view. Listening from a truly unlocked mind means being willing to mull over the other side of the argument, and if it makes sense, go along with it, be willing to give it a shot.

R. Gopalkrishnan (Director Tata Sons and ex-Vice Chairman, Hindustan Levers Ltd) recounts that at 27, when he was appointed Brand Manager for Lifebuoy and Pears soap, he found to his chagrin that he could not move a pin without checking with his seniors. One day he gently expressed his frustration to his marketing director and asked whether he could not be given total charge.

The marketing director smiled and replied, "The perception and reality are both right. You will get total charge when you know more about the brand than anyone else in the company—about its formulation, raw materials, production cost, consumer's perceptions, distribution and so on. How long do you think it will take?"

"Maybe ten years," Gopalkrishnan replied, "and I don't expect to be the Lifebuoy and Pears Brand Manager for so long!"

We tend to chafe under 'bureaucratic red tape of behemoth organisations' and 'over-conservatism of the seniors'. Instead,

Keep in mind the boss's different communication styles.

Gopalkrishnan accepted his lesson of 'deserve before you desire' with humility and grace.

One reason why we resist being hundred per cent receptive to another outlook is that it means giving up our own idea. To many of us, it becomes synonymous with our identity, and 'losing' this round means losing the very self, which is unacceptable to the ego! Instead of resisting an opposite point of view, if we can say, "Let me examine it more closely as there may be something worthwhile in it"—that is openness. It is Neils Bohr, the famous physicist, who once said, "The opposite of fact may well be fiction, but the opposite of a profound truth may well be another profound truth."

Building bridges of communication with the boss.

Demonstrate you are listening

While openness is vital to construction of communication bridges, it is equally important to demonstrate receptivity. Listen and keep listening. Even if the other person has a different point of view, listening shows respect and good intentions, and will make the other person feel valued. Body language plays an important role, because every gesture is a powerful visual clue of our response, which the others are quick to pick up, albeit at the subconscious level.

While communicating with your boss, some examples of positive signals of interest and confidence are:

- Looking at your boss and slightly leaning into the conversation.
- Eye contact, nodding and smiling shows your boss that you are involved and interested in his views.
- Tone of voice which is even, calm, and not high pitched or breathless.

Some gestures to avoid as you speak:

- Leg shaking or foot tapping–rhythmic movement of any periphery of the body indicates restlessness, nervousness or boredom.
- Other fidgeting movements like playing with your hair, touching your face, stroking your neck could indicate self-doubt or nervousness.
- Tightly crossed arms–as they 'close' or 'protect' your body, you come across as being closed, as opposed to openly sharing and receiving different points of views.
- Shoulder shrug–it says you don't believe what you just said.

Paraphrasing or reflecting skills

Verbally, you indicate your receptivity by occasionally paraphrasing or repeating in your own words what you have understood of what the other person said. The best way to paraphrase is to listen carefully to what the other person is saying. You could use initial phrases, such as

- "In other words..."
- "So what you are saying is...."
- "I gather that..."
- "If I understand what you are saying..."

It helps confirm you are on the same track, and also communicates to the other person that you are 'with him'.

We transmit personal, non-verbal signals all the time. They reflect our attitudes/responses to a situation.

Importance of body language

When we are speaking, we need to be aware that our body is sending messages constantly. At any given time, we are sending signals about ourselves through every little gesture (the way we stand, touch our nose, scratch our head, fidget with hands, jiggle our foot, make eye-contact or shift our gaze). Our body language is said to be a leak of what is actually happening inside us.

Considerable research has gone in the understanding of non-verbal communication since the 1960s. One person who has been credited with pioneering work is Dr Albert Mehrabian (currently

Professor of Psychology at University of California, Los Angeles) who established the data for the effectiveness of spoken communications:

- 7 per cent of meaning is in the words that are spoken.
- 38 per cent of meaning is in the tone of the voice.
- 55 per cent of meaning in facial expression and body gestures.

Even while Mehrabian's model has become one of the most widely referenced statistics in communications, it does evoke surprise. Did you realise that the non-verbal component has an influence to the extent of 97 per cent in the overall effectiveness of communication? The impact however cannot be denied—consider the results of the following experiment: A man was made to cross a traffic light at the wrong moment, when the signal was still red. Interestingly, it was found that a larger number of pedestrians followed him when he was dressed in a business suit and tie, than when he was dressed casually!

The experiment illustrates that people associate authority with the business suit. We can say (certainly initial) perceptions do result from appearances, which is part of the 55 per cent impact through body language. Neatly ironed clothes and well-polished shoes do send out a message, "I feel good about myself and my work, and I am a winner."

Does this mean that form is more important than content? The answer is no, but if you don't pay attention to the 97 per cent, the impact of your message could well be diluted, or even lost.

Don't know where you stand with the boss? Ask for feedback

One of the commonest complaints subordinates have is, "I don't know where I stand with my boss, because he doesn't give me any feedback", or "The only pointer I get is when things aren't going well, or there is a problem".

Many bosses do avoid confronting unsatisfactory performance issues for fear of creating misunderstandings or ill will, which they believe will result in de-motivation and lowered morale. Instead of sharing of thoughts directly and clearly, they ignore the matter, hoping the junior will 'catch on'.

Perhaps the boss's fear of the junior's inability to accept criticism is based on a previous experience of the latter not taking it well. But this avoidance means heavy costs to both sides. One outcome is dissatisfaction at the end of the year, as a gap is shown between the boss's rating and the employee's expectation. The other is that the employee's shortcomings are a blind spot for him, hampering his own growth. So instead of leaving it to chance, or your boss, seek out feedback when you finish a substantial piece of work by asking specific questions:

- "What do you think of the report?"
- "How do you think the presentation to the management committee went on the new product launch?"

Your reaction to feedback

Many of us ask for feedback, anticipating and hoping to hear only good things. In such a case, the unspoken expectation is often sensed, and the response suitably given, which is not of much use! (Once we were at a restaurant, where the chef came and asked, "I hope everything is okay?" The question was phrased in a manner that left us little choice but to say, 'yes!' It didn't really solicit a descriptive answer, so we nodded our heads and smiled... not much feedback for him there!). So if you are really open, and ask open-ended questions, your chances of hearing meaningful feedback increase.

Even with preparedness, hearing negative comments can be unpleasant and hurtful. The SAD-FAD outlined below is a useful sequence which helps in handling feedback. The first stage is to understand negative feelings we experience (SAD), which are natural. However, to get to the meaningful and useful parts, we need to put them behind us and move to the next stage of listening and asking questions (FAD).

Table 8

Stage I: Our normal reaction to criticism	S	**Surprise, shock**
	A	Feeling **angry**, annoyed, irritated and impatient
	D	**Defensiveness**–giving reasons, explanations, excuses
Stage II: What we need to do	F	**Force** yourself to hear out the other person
	A	**Ask** probing questions
	D	Find out what you must do **differently**

SAD

When we receive negative feedback, the first reactions are feelings of **surprise, shock**, followed by **anger** and irritation. We tend to become **defensive**, and there is a tendency to dismiss the feedback by rationalising, such as,

- "He's too far removed from the situation to have a proper perspective," or
- "In such a short time what else could they expect?" or
- "He didn't brief me properly".

Reaching the last stage, which is accepting what is useful, can be only reached if the SAD is dealt with awareness and maturity. It requires that we acknowledge our feelings to ourselves, but remain quiet, allowing space for the feedback-giver to finish speaking. Many of us get stuck here, never reaching the second stage at all.

SAD – FAD helps us in handling feedback.

FAD

We can get distracted by judgemental feedback like:

- "That was not well handled. You really need to pull up your socks there."
- "The design you submitted is not up to the mark."

We need to **force** ourselves to listen out, **asking** follow-up probing questions (to clarify the situation) like:

- "I'm sorry, you feel that way. Can you give me one or two examples to help me understand the problem areas?"

- "I'm sorry, you weren't satisfied. Can I check with you if the problem was density of errors, or was it the format? Or anything else?"
- "Can I request you to explain which parts are not clear, or are missing?"

After you have drawn out from the person everything he could possibly have to say, close with, "Do you have any advice on how I could have handled it **differently**?" This question helps to turn the conversation into a constructive mode.

Continue asking questions gently and calmly if the suggestion is not plausible or impractical or flawed, until you have determined in your mind—what needed to be changed, what could be changed, and what need not have been changed.

Be open and transparent: Don't withhold information

"Who am I to withhold information?" you might ask. It's the boss who doesn't share the big picture, or 'forgets' to give the changed specifications on time, or inform about decisions that were taken 'upstairs'. That's the reason of all problems including last-minute panic buttons, resulting in late working and upset schedules. Well, we know that the boss is the boss, let's look at what the effective subordinate should not be doing.

There could be two situations of subordinates withholding relevant data from the boss. One, where they intentionally sit on news they have had access to, perhaps through the unofficial route. This is often in the case of relationships turned sour or antagonistic. It's a subtle, indirect, underhand way of 'getting even'. Or say, the boss's boss calls the subordinate for a brief or update (perhaps in boss's absence). The opportunity for one-upmanship by not keeping the boss updated becomes too much to give up. Needles to say, the cold war escalates.

The other is whenever there has been a goof-up or faulty

judgement. Remember the boss doesn't like surprises. In the words of Peter Drucker, "Never try to brush an elephant under the rug."

Raghu, the factory manager, of a pen-manufacturing unit shares his experience:

"We were all set to launch a new product. The Chairman-cum-Managing Director arrived from the head office to formally inaugurate the production process—he was to press a button and the machine would roll out the pens. Even as it started, someone pointed out, 'The pen caps are too tight!' The problem was assigned to some technical fault, and the CMD left after expressing his displeasure.

"To get to the bottom of the problem, I studied all the working sheets, standard operating procedures, original samples, and realised that we had used the wrong polypropylene (raw material composition) for the cap! My colleagues and even seniors advised me to sweep it under the carpet, but I decided to seek an appointment with CMD and make a clean breast.

"Armed with calculations of damaged stock as well as recovery plan, I entered the lion's den. He was understandably furious. It took several weeks for things to smoothen out, but I have no regrets. I know it was the right thing to do, than to wait one day for the bomb to explode."

Make your boss look good

While you don't have to be as heavy handed about it as the villain's side-kick or *chamcha* of Hindi films, being supportive of your boss does set a positive tone to the relationship. Always be seen upholding a positive image of your boss, which will enhance your credibility and that of your department. In front of others, mention the pluses and the strengths, and be seen as your boss's champion.

Everyone likes to be complimented (yes, including the boss, as he too is a member of the human species—much as we would like to believe differently!). Occasional responsibility-related praise (giving credit for specific contributions) sounds authentic and works well, even with the dourest of boss types! For example,

- "That bit of astute negotiation really turned the tables in our discussions today," or
- "It was a great ideas to address the staff spouses, it really bowled them over!" or
- "The idea you came up with last week..."

Of course, there are people who are blatant about it and don't mind doing the puppy act—staying late if the boss is sitting late, following the boss out for a smoke, laughing at all his jokes, the works. Unfortunately, studies show that apple polishing works in gaining favour with your boss. But in the bottom line, it is possible to maintain both your integrity and positive intent by not withholding a sincere compliment.

One ground rule that cannot be over-emphasised is *don't bad-mouth your boss under any circumstances.* It is tempting to look for proof of your own poor opinion of the boss in discussion with others. You get a short-lived and false feeling of 'getting back at him', but it will always haunt you because your enemies will make sure he hears the juicy bits. Plus, it will do more harm to you than to him, as others will also lose trust in you. Complaining, criticising and cribbing does nothing but spiral the negativity in you, around you, eating you and the work atmosphere like cancer.

6

Assertiveness Skills: Communicating Confidently and Respectfully

We have seen that communication with the boss is as important as a lubricant is for our car engine. Without it our career would sputter and stall, and work-life would be full of breakdowns and headaches. In the next few chapters we will take some examples of situations, which, if not clarified, have the potential to worsen our irritation with time. We will see how to address them calmly and reasonably without rubbing the boss the wrong way, without demanding, yet getting our point across.

What are some of these typical work situations? When we need to

- present an idea or suggestion;
- clarify expectations and goals;
- make a request or ask for resources;
- disagree with the boss;
- bring up any other difficult or sensitive issue bothering us.

Why do we tend to stay quiet and push things under the rug?

There are several reasons why many of us choose not to speak up:

We expect the boss to be a mind-reader

We tend to overlook a simple but obvious fact–the boss does not have a silicon chip in his brain, which can beam into ours and read our mind! We mistakenly assume that what is obvious to us should be obvious to him as well.

- "Isn't it his responsibility to give clear instructions and guidelines when he delegates a task to me? He should know with my two years' experience I need more handholding..."
- "Isn't it obvious that we need XY equipment before this project can be completed?"
- " If the boss is not doing anything about it, it means he can't or won't."

However, unless you tell him about your ideas, challenges, problems, yes, even achievements, we will be working with shadows of assumptions—"I imagine the boss knows."

We operate from an unquestioned assumption, "I have no choice"

Sometimes it doesn't even occur to us that we can speak up in a frank and respectful manner. For one, there is an apprehension, "Even if I speak, how do I handle the communication? I'm positive, I'll mess it up." The fear could be based on a past negative experience with the same or a different boss, who growled at you or who never seemed to have the time to talk to you. It could also be based on assumptions: "It will be considered improper to speak up" or "I will be misunderstood" or "There will be negative repercussions later."

We are afraid of accountability

Another reason is the fear to take the steering wheel of our lives in our own hands. To own responsibility means to admit that mistakes and failures (of not delivering, or missed promotion, or poor relationship with boss) have been contributed at least in part by me. It requires courage to accept it, and then a huge effort to rectify matters. Isn't it easier to just close our eyes and take the support of a comforting pillow of laying blame on externals like bad luck, office politics, inconsiderate boss, downturn in the economy, poor job market, etc.?

Responses can be categorised as passive, aggressive and assertive behaviour

What is passive behaviour?

"After one of my bosses gives me dictation, I show her the transcribed draft on which she makes corrections. I type it onto the letterhead for her signature, but often she makes corrections again, and yet again, requiring me to make the 'final copy' two times or more. I feel it's a waste of time, which if we avoid, I can get more work done. But I would never dream of raising this with her."

—*Reena Mazumdar, Secretary to the CFO*

"My boss has a habit of giving me 'urgent' deadlines. On the last two occasions, I wrestled with it till midnight, and felt a sense of accomplishment when I executed it and handed it over on time. Guess what he did—he put it away and didn't look at it for two days! You can imagine how deflated and disappointed I felt. But what can I do? I know this will happen again, and I feel trapped."

—*Alok Jaideep, Team Leader (at a Call Centre)*

"There are times when my boss abdicates rather than delegates a task. In the first place the deadlines are really stretched, and over it, project specifications are constantly changing. In the product I am developing, there were two rounds of changing the code...With my two years of experience, I feel lost and overwhelmed..."

—*Sudhir Tailang, Software Engineer*

A passive or submissive response is when people:

- don't speak up even when something is bothering them;
- allow the problem to gnaw and eat away their insides even as they fret and fume;
- let themselves be pushed—they don't check back on whether deadlines or project requirements can be negotiated or worked out;
- assume others' rights are more important than their own ("Who am I to say anything to the boss?");
- want to avoid conflicts at all costs;
- don't honestly acknowledge their own needs and feelings.

The passive style is adopted because we are brought up on a diet of don'ts: Don't complain; don't make mistakes; better let sleeping dogs lie; don't upset the apple cart; don't take risks; don't make others angry; don't question things. Obeying these rules avoids conflicts, but we pay a price—the price of reduced self-respect, personal unhappiness, and increased feelings of helplessness and lack of control.

Typical passive behaviours are:

- hesitation in contributing own ideas, which are believed not to be of much value (or expressing them in a timid or apologetic manner);
- having a constant hum of anxiety in the mind about too much work and pending assignments;

The passive style is adopted because we are brought up on a diet of dont's.

- body language consisting of:
  - evasive eye contact (looking down at feet to avoid expressing feelings);
  - fidgeting nervously;
  - hesitant, over-soft voice, often dull and monotonous;
  - hunching shoulders, arms crossed for protection.
- Use of tentative sounds/ phrases like "Uh uh...", throat clearing, "Hmmm...", "sort of", as well as expressions which convey diffidence like "It's not important really..." "It doesn't matter..."

What is aggressive behaviour?

Aggressive behaviour is when people at the workplace (*see* 'Bosses who Harass and Terrorise' (Chapter 10):

- are authoritarian and rarely listen to another's point of view;
- rigidly stick to their views without compromise;
- push juniors into accepting impossible or unrealistic deadlines/ work-loads;
- want their own way, even if it means trampling on others;
- want a person or situation to be different from what it inherently is;
- express thoughts, feelings or beliefs in unacceptable and unsuitable ways with the belief they are right.

Typical aggressive behaviours are:

- putting others down (in front of colleagues), being condescending or showing disdain: "You must be joking", "You must have been asleep when you prepared this…";
- blaming other people or outside factors "It was your fault..", "You said…";
- manipulating to get your own way;
- body language consisting of:
  - staring or dominating eye contact;
  - sarcastic, cold, hard tone which is very firm, often shouting;
  - standing or striding around with head in air;
  - fist thumping and finger pointing;
  - eyebrows raised in incredulity or scepticism.

The aggressive style pushes people around without concern for their feelings. In the short term they get their own way, but in the long term nobody wants to be around them! It leaves others with feelings of being controlled, inadequate, embarrassed and losing power. Managers can lose respect of their subordinates, missing out on important ideas and information. Another problem with aggressive behaviour is that it can also trigger an angry or hostile response from others, deteriorating the situation further. (So while aggressive behaviour is more commonly seen in the boss than in the subordinate, occasionally a junior could react by not following instructions or match rudeness for rudeness.)

Why is the fight/flight response so common?

Millions of years ago in prehistoric times, when man lived in caves and wilderness, to survive the aggression of beasts, humans and other elements, he had to attack back (fight) or hide and run (flight). Today, survival messages written in our genes haven't been erased, and reaction patterns are the same when triggered by a situation creating anxiety. However, this reactive reaction is no longer appropriate or helpful, and is called an *emotional hijack*. Man needs to teach himself to respond more rationally to use his mind (and not his gut), to think, and then act. This is a proactive or assertive approach.

What is assertive behaviour?

Assertiveness is the middle ground between aggression and passivity. It is about reasonable behaviour and finding solutions that suit both the sides. Assertiveness means:

- acknowledging your own feelings to yourself ("*My boss gives me bits and pieces of tasks without total responsibility of the entire project, and I am feeling restless and unfulfilled*");
- understanding you have a right to (professional) respect, at the same time owing respect to the other person;
- having a right to speak your mind and ask for what you want;
- being clear about what you want (which is reasonable and fair);
- understanding it is up to you to give a best shot to manage an unsatisfactory situation;

- communicating your point calmly, openly and confidently;
- understanding what situations you can and can't change.

Typical assertive behaviours are:

- stating our thoughts clearly and confidently, without making demands or belittling ourselves;
- coping with justified criticism, and being able to give it when required in a considerate and balanced manner;
- body language consisting of:
  - steady eye contact;
  - open body posture (without crossed arms), sitting upright and relaxed;

Neither fight nor flight response is helpful.

- head held straight;
- appropriate facial expression—smiling when relaxed or satisfied, frowning when displeased;

- making statements that are brief and to the point;
- asking open-ended questions to get others' views: "What do you think?" or "What can we do to resolve this?"
- being clear and direct by using 'I' statements, e.g. "I think", "I want", "I believe".

Tips for practising assertiveness

1. ***Don't weaken your communication by apologising, making excuses or giving long explanations.*** When we use expressions like, "I'm sorry to bring this up..", "Maybe...", "Would you mind very much..." we are making our message feeble, thus undermining ourselves, making it easier for others to disregard or dismiss.
2. ***Be brief.*** The fewer words you use, the bigger the impact. A rule of thumb is to listen more often than speak. Observe senior people around you—many powerful and effective people communicate with a few, well-chosen words.
3. ***Present yourself confidently.*** Look at the person in the eye; hold your body upright and consciously relax your shoulders. Keep your face calm. Speak in a normal tone –without shouting or whispering.
4. ***Plan and rehearse what you will say.*** In potentially difficult situations, successful people report going to the extent of even writing down their 'script'. (The next section provides guidelines and examples of how to use A. FISH).
5. ***Watch your timing!*** Choose the correct moment to bring up sensitive issues. Wrong times to go to the boss for example are: Just as he is about to leave for a vacation, he is about to step out for lunch, he is in the middle of a high-pressure deadline, or has just been rapped on the knuckles by his boss!
6. ***You must be in the driver's seat.*** The initiative to bring up and discuss issues (whether making a suggestion, asking for clarification, or asking for resources) must be yours. *You* should decide when you want to bring up the issue rather than wait for the boss to ask or an explosion to happen.

Assertiveness is the middle ground between aggressive and submissive behaviour.

7. ***After adequate preparations, have the courage to say your piece!***

In short, assertiveness is about being a more effective person.

Assertive behaviour doesn't come naturally, and to practise it is not easy. It is also important to accept that once in a while, when we goof up, that is, lose control and balance, it's okay. After all, nobody is perfect, and to berate ourselves when a mistake is made is again bullying behaviour–here we are bullying ourselves! After learning our lesson, we have to forgive ourselves and move on.

Assertive behaviour is not very commonly seen. When we practise it, the other party could feel temporarily disconcerted. But remember, assertiveness is not about winning a popularity contest. If we are convinced our actions and words are fair (to ourselves and others), our self-respect and self-confidence will rise.

Table 9

A	Alert the other person if something important is going to be discussed, e.g. "Do you have 10 minutes? There's something important I'd like to discuss with you."
F	Describe the facts of the situation in simple, specific, unemotional terms.
I	Make an 'I' statement expressing your feelings. Say what you think/feel, • share concern, ask for help; • link to other's concerns/ feelings.
S	Put forward your solutions, suggestions, wants or needs in specific and reasonable terms. Point out benefits. If required, do your homework in advance, be it to collect data, make calculations, etc. to support your points.
H	Hear the person out, patiently and respectfully! If required, repeat your point.

Assertiveness guidelines: A preplanned script

An important aspect of staying balanced and centred is to anticipate situations, and plan in advance what we are going to say. Doing our homework is thus an integral part of learning to be assertive, which includes working out what is the (win-win) outcome we would want. This also consists of preparing our

A FISH is a helpful format to put across your point of view in a (sensitive) situation.

reply for various eventualities: Refusal, resistance, rejection or further questions.

Here is a helpful format to use when putting your point of view in a (sensitive) situation in an easy to remember acronym: A. FISH.

Let's revisit Reena Mazumdar's example we saw earlier. "After one of my bosses gives me dictation, I show her the transcribed draft on which she makes corrections. I type it on to the letterhead for her signature, but often she makes corrections again, and yet again, requiring me to make the 'final copy' two times or more. I feel it's a waste of time, which if we can avoid, I can get more done. But I would never dream of raising this with her." Her response is passive, because let alone expressing her thoughts and concerns to her boss, it has not even occurred to her to bring it up.

After she learnt about assertiveness, Reena decided speak to her boss using A. FISH guidelines:

Table 10

A **Alert** other person	*Do you have 10 minutes? There's a problem I need your help with.*
F Describe the **facts**.	*It's about typing letters. I do realise that drafting a letter takes time and effort. After you have corrected the initial draft, often I have to correct and print out the same letter twice or thrice, due to a second round of corrections.*
I **I** statement expressing your feelings, concerns.	*I feel it's not using my time well as yours effectively, as I have to come to you repeatedly for corrections.*
S Put forward your **solutions**, point out benefits.	*Can I suggest something? If all corrections could be made in the first draft itself, I would be able to complete 10 to 15 per cent of more typing work in one day.*
H **Hear** the person out.	*Could we try it out for a week?*

She ended the conversation, thanking her boss for hearing her out.

Communicate from other's point of view

We frequently talk from an egocentric point of view. We build an idea or project mainly in terms of what makes sense to us. However, when we are communicating, we must not forget we are seeking to influence and persuade. To get the other person to see our outlook, we need to 'sell' its benefit, so we must frame it in his context.

To illustrate this, let's go back to Sudhir Tailang's example and see how the conversation went when he discussed this with the boss.

"There are times when my boss abdicates rather than delegates a task. In the first place the deadlines are really stretched, and over it, project specifications are constantly changing. In the product I am developing, there have already been two rounds of changing the code... With my two years of experience, I feel lost and overwhelmed..."

—Sudhir Tailang, Software Engineer

Table 11

A Alert other person.	*I want to speak to your about my work. Do you have 15 minutes, sir?*
F Describe the facts	*The project I'm working on is constantly changing scope, and we have already had two rounds of changing the code.*
Boss: But it's the customer's requirement. We can't help it, can we?	
I I statement expressing your feelings, concerns.	*Yes sir, I understand. The deadline is also so tight; I am feeling squeezed and pressurised, as though everything is out of control...*

<table>
<tr><td colspan="2">Boss: This experience is exactly what you need–it will add value to your learning!</td></tr>
<tr><td>S1
Put forward your <u>solutions</u>, point out the benefits.</td><td>Yes sir, I appreciate that. But since I am new and inexperienced, can we review deadlines, and extend it by three to four days?</td></tr>
<tr><td colspan="2">Boss: I'm sorry, you'll have to come on weekends and complete it, like everyone else.</td></tr>
<tr><td>S2
Put forward your <u>solutions</u>, point out the benefits.</td><td>It is not possible, sir. Can I make another suggestion? Can you help by assigning another developer to check the codes, so that I feel more confident about their accuracy?</td></tr>
<tr><td colspan="2">Boss: Hmm... We could think of that...</td></tr>
<tr><td>H
<u>Hear</u> the person out/close</td><td>Thanks a lot, sir.</td></tr>
</table>

What Sudhir handled well:

He had thought out the specific outcomes he wanted, and had in his mind two solutions. In this case the boss didn't agree to the first (S1- extension of deadline), but was amenable to the second (S2- additional resources in the form of another developer).

What Sudhir didn't do well:

1. Instead of presenting his case from his own reference point "since I am new and inexperienced" (see S1), Sudhir would do better to speak from his boss's viewpoint, "*In the interest of giving the best quality to the customer and making it totally bug proof, can I suggest that...*" Why? Because, one, the boss doesn't care about

Sudhir's difficulties – he is concerned with the outcome, the end result. Two, Sudhir is undermining himself by pointing out his own weakness or lack of experience.

2. Avoid the phrase, "*It's not possible*" when talking to the boss! Present data, alternatives, but don't say 'no'.
3. Sudhir also should have closed the conversation at the end by getting a commitment from the boss regarding the developer that would be assigned to check the codes. "*That would be great, sir. How much time would he be able to give to this project, and when will he start?*"

Does assertiveness always get results?

Assertiveness is not easy and it is not effortless. Even with practice and exertion, does it always get you the desired results? The answer is 'no.'

Here is P.C. Dutta's experience. *On the day before Diwali, Dutta was planning to leave work on time at 5.30 p.m. as he had promised to take his wife and child to complete festival purchases. Being busy in the preceding days, this was a long pending and looked forward to event by his family. However, at 3 p.m. his boss walked in and handed him a presentation to complete for their overseas buyers, whose programme had suddenly changed—they were now arriving on the day after Diwali. This meant at least six to seven hours of work for Dutta today. Dutta was dismayed (and annoyed), but decided to give it his assertive best.* Using A.FISH, he said,

A : (Alert the other person) *About the presentation for our buyers.*

F : (Facts) *I do, of course understand this is high priority work: I have an important family commitment today evening.*

I. (I statement) *and I would find it very difficult to work late tonight.*

Assertiveness may not always get the results you want, but it will leave you with a feeling of self-respect.

S : (Solution) *Can I request that I come the day after Diwali, early in the morning at 7.30 a.m. and give it to you by 3 p.m.?*

H : (Hear out the other person) *Will that work for you?*

However, the boss said (also assertively), "I do understand your problem, but I am afraid we have no choice here. I can't leave it to the last moment, as we will need to go through a dry run in the morning after Diwali. There may also be some editing requirement. I would like to see it tonight before I leave."

What were Dutta's options? To stay back, of course (if he

wants a career with this company). Loyalty to his boss and commitment to work are priority, and sacrifices have to be made at times. He called his family and explained the exigency, and he would make it to them the following day.

So, was assertiveness of no use? Would it have been better to say nothing to his boss? Dutta felt that having spoken up led to three benefits for him:

1. Earning brownie points from the boss for having made a sacrifice and giving up the family's evening, that too with cheerful acceptance.
2. Sending a discreet message that Dutta was not a pushover for unplanned/aggressive/unreasonable demands at the nth hour.
3. A feeling of self-respect for having "spoken-up" and not remained a mouse frightened of his boss's shadow.

Quiz: Are you submissive, aggressive or assertive with your boss?

Below are listed ten situations typically encountered in an office situation. As you read on, tick the alternative most indicative of the way you would react. After you have responded honestly, turn to the end of this questionnaire to score yourself, to get an idea of the style you largely tend to adopt.

1. You are in charge of a new project. Due to uncertainties in the environment, it was put on hold for the past one week. Suddenly, your boss gives the green signal, and expects you to adhere to all previous deadlines. You
   a. send out a strong memo saying, "It is impossible";
   b. keep quiet, as you don't like being outspoken or bring up controversial issues;
   c. send a courteous but firm note reminding the time loss due to the project being put on hold, and requesting extension of eight days.
2. You are attending a two-day in-house workshop on 'Interpersonal Skills', organised by the HR Department, which you are finding

useful. Halfway through, you receive a message that your boss wants you back due to some urgent work. You

a. leave immediately, after informing the faculty, but are feeling irritated and resentful;

b. call the boss and explain your staying and completing the course has value for you and your department, and offer to come early next morning and finish the task;

c. ask the HR head to speak to your boss (as you know she feels strongly about this issue of people being pulled away from a training programme).

3. As a new (relatively junior) member of a project team, you find a project update meeting is held every month, which you have not been asked to attend so far. This is your third month of joining the team, and you are feeling left out at not being invited for this meeting. You

   a. bite your lip and say nothing. Maybe 'they' feel at your level you don't have much to contribute;

   b. meet the Project Leader and request if you can be allowed to attend, as it would enable you to understand the "big picture" and help you contribute in a more meaningful way;

   c. burst out with, "How am I to know? Ask the people who attend the project update meeting", when the Project Leader asks you the status of some part of the project.

4. When you go into your boss's room for discussions, you end up waiting for long periods of time as he receives phone calls. You

   a. politely explain to him this situation is causing you discomfort, and request if he can switch his cellphone off for 20 minutes of your meeting time;

   b. one day you can't contain yourself and walk out, even though your boss had gestured for you to wait;

   c. fret and fume at this waste of time, but feel you are in no position to say anything. After all he's the boss.

5. You have been overloaded with work for the last couple of months, and are feeling very pressurised right now with pending deadlines, unanswered mail, etc. Suddenly your boss pops in and asks you to collate some 'urgent' data 'right-away'. You say,

a. "I don't know anything about this data. Let me first streamline my work then I'll see";

b. "Okay, fine," but are inwardly gnashing your teeth;

c. "You have asked for the Hamlin Report by tomorrow morning and the vendor-rating summary by tomorrow evening. If I work on this data, everything shifts by half-day, is that okay?"

6. You have really slogged over a proposal outlining a new approach for Employee Reward Scheme, which your boss wanted by a certain date. A week later, you seek his feedback and find he hasn't even read it! You say

   a. "I know you're so busy that you can't be bothered about such trivial things. Should we scrap it?";

   b. "It's alright, it's not so important anyway";

   c. "I am disappointed you haven't read it, as it is important for the employee morale. It should ideally be launched with the objective-setting process within ten days. When can we fix time to discuss it?"

7. You have been sanctioned two weeks (long overdue) leave and you are planning to travel to your hometown and have already booked train tickets. Two days before your leave starts, your boss's boss, Mr Bali says, "You can't go on leave as Rajiv (your boss) in on tour. This project is too important to leave unattended." Rajiv is due to return five days from now. You

   a. feel helpless and bitter, crib to your colleagues and family and make arrangements to cancel train bookings;

   b. phone Rajiv and convince him that you will leave a detailed brief on project status, which will make it possible for him to continue from where you have left. Reverting to Mr Bali, you explain how you have coordinated with Rajiv, and request him permission to leave as originally planned;

   c. have taken leave after three years, have slogged for the company, and are now very upset. You tell Mr Bali you can't change your plan, and offer to resign.

8. You want to apply for a colleague's job who has recently resigned. You

a. ask for a meeting with your boss where you would go prepared to "pitch" your case;

b. although you drop hints to your boss about this position, you feel it will be too over-ambitious to push your case, and decide to wait until he brings it up, or see it posted as an internal vacancy;

c. walk into your boss's office and express your frustration at not being considered for this vacancy.

9. The project you are working on requires about 30 pages of documentation—by far too excessive with unnecessary components. You

   a. feel it's a bother and a waste of time, but do it as your boss has asked for it;

   b. ask for old files to study the original formats of standard norms and procedures for documentation of similar projects, and find that 15 pages cover this. You take it for discussion with your boss;

   c. you decide it's not worth your bother to waste your time on this "periphery work" and push it to one of your junior team members.

10. As a cost-cutting measure, your unit has decided to stop all overtime. Suddenly there is an 'urgent' order from MD's office to be processed and shipped out. You

    a. immediately give instructions for the production to start, even at the cost of high overtime, as the order has come from the MD's office and can't be questioned.

    b. send out an e-mail to MD's Executive Assistant saying there is no way that "no overtime" norms are going to be violated, and that the order cannot be processed.

    c. pick up the phone to find out from the MD's Executive Assistant when is the exact deadline for meeting this requirement, and whether it can be extended by a day, pointing out the expenses the company will be saving.

Scoring yourself: Circle your choice and count the number of choices in each column. The column with the maximum score indicates your predominant response style: Whether you are able to maintain your inner balance and stay assertive, or become a human doormat, or an elephant on the rampage.

Table 12

	Submissive	*Aggressive*	*Assertive*
1.	b	a	c
2.	a	c	b
3.	a	c	b
4.	c	b	a
5.	b	a	c
6.	b	a	c
7.	a	c	b
8.	b	c	a
9.	a	c	b
10.	a	b	c
Your score			

What your score means

Assertive behaviour: You know what you want and have the confidence to put your point of view across, rather than caving in to authority, or hoping that others will guess what is on your mind. When you face problems or things bother you, you say what you think and feel, calmly and clearly, without offending or demanding.

Your assertive approach allows you to handle difficult situations effectively, at the same time judge what situations you can and can't influence. It helps you to control the way you feel about your work, your boss, rather than attempt to control them.

Passive behaviour: You tend to go along with the flow of things, assuming that you don't have any rights, hesitating to share your views and making no attempt to state your position.

Even when you do state your view, it is so half-hearted that others disregard them. In the short term, it reduces anxiety as you avoid conflict, but in the long run it erodes your self-respect as you end up feeling anxious about having taken on too much, and having let yourself down.

Another characteristic of passive or unassertive people is that they hope they'll get what they want, but expect others to guess their wishes. As a result they often end up feeling angry with others, and think they should somehow have known what was wanted.

Aggressive behaviour: You tend to express your own needs, wants, opinions as a demand—in inappropriate ways like sarcasm, abrasive words, loosing one's temper, etc. It is a rare subordinate who behaves aggressively with his boss. It is likely to happen if the subordinate has been passive for a long time—not bringing up issues, which are bothering him and swallowing his discomfort. One day the dam bursts, and the reaction comes out like an uncontrolled outburst. It may leave you with temporary feelings of elation and power, but in the long-term it results in deterioration of relations.

7

Finding My Inner Balance: Removing Doubts, Fears and Negative Emotions

Have you ever experienced

- hesitation in expressing your views at the workplace – to the boss, in a meeting, etc. (for fear of being rejected or ridiculed)?
- difficulty in voicing disagreement with others' views, especially a senior? (what if he starts disliking me)?
- high anxiety levels in conflict situations?
- annoyance when being given feedback, especially negative feedback? (who is he to say this to me?)
- anger at a perceived injustice, and frustration at 'having' to swallow it?
- losing your cool (by losing temper, shouting or becoming aggressive), and later regretting it?

While these negative emotions and self-doubts are normal human reactions, they do get in the way of our effectiveness at work. What is the root cause? How can we battle and conquer these problems?

Maintaining my inner balance

Have you seen a toy—a rotund, colourful doll that babies and little children are given to play with? It has a smiling face sitting on a spherical base. It's centre of gravity is so positioned that every time it is pushed, it sways to and fro, accompanied by a little tinkling sound, and regains its original position, without toppling over.

The question to reflect upon is: How balanced are we? What does it take to knock out our equilibrium? How much of ballast is there in our central core that gives us our stability, or inner balance? Does a little shove tip us over, causing us to react by either losing our cool, or by withdrawing like the proverbial tortoise?

- "The boss never listens, so what's the point in trying?"
- "I feel like a football which is being kicked around, but what can I do?"
- "His absurdity made me lose my temper."
- "She was shouting so I had to shout back."

When we make any of the above statements we are reacting from either helplessness/victim position ("poor me"), or aggressor/persecutor position ("I'll show you" or "How dare you"). Assertiveness helps us understand that while we can't change the situation, we can change our feelings towards it. We have a choice of accessing our inner balance. It is only then that we gain mastery over ourselves, when the response is not a reaction to the other person, but a measured and considered comeback of our choice. We can choose to speak calmly, or if the situation demands, remain quiet, and if it is best for us we can even express stronger emotions.

Where does this inner balance come from? Its origin lies in our self-esteem. It is the evaluation—high or low—we make and

With conscious effort and practice it is possible to maintain our inner balance.

hold of ourselves. It is based on how capable, likable or successful we consider ourselves to be. With a shaky self-esteem we feel uneasy and insecure when a difficult or conflict-creating situation arises. We feel threatened that we will be swept along or overwhelmed by the situation and the people in it, and this causes us to either flare up and hit out (aggression) or withdraw and become a doormat (submission).

Inner balance comes from self-esteem

Self-esteem is the single most important factor in how we communicate and relate with others. It is a demon we all battle with at some point in our lives. It is how we feel about ourselves, deep down inside us. It is the sum total of our own view of ourselves based on past experiences of success and failure, our value system, what we do, what we are, what we have. In other words, more than what others think of us, it is what we think of ourselves.

It is a filter we have created around us which causes us to interpret (see, hear, evaluate and understand) messages and inputs we receive. A weak or fragile self-esteem causes difficulty in dealing with negative feedback, criticism, or failure (all of which are necessary and inevitable parts of life), which we associate with 'losing face'. Self-esteem in this case is at the mercy of others/ external situations.

How does self-esteem develop?

Self-esteem develops as a result of how others treat us. But in turn, that depends on how we value ourselves, because we unconsciously send out subtle signals of our self-rating (*see* Body Language section in Chapter 5). Others quickly pick up indications of low self-worth and treat us accordingly! So it's like the chicken and egg story.

However, its origin lies in childhood experiences with important people in our lives—sometimes called 'significant others' (parents, teachers, relatives and grandparents). Feelings of 'not okay' arise in either of the two situations: We received a lot of criticism and non-acceptance (messages of "you are not good enough"); or we had over-indulgent and over-protective parents who gave too much praise/ rewards too easily, even when it was not warranted. It results in a wide gap between what "we are" and what "we should be".

For example, when Kanti Das was growing up, he was constantly compared with his cousins who were academically

A fragile or weak self-esteem comes from lack of self-acceptance.

brighter. When he wanted to switch to Arts stream, his father convinced him to pursue science, and later pressurised him to sit for competitive entrance exams. He, of course, wasn't capable of clearing any. Today, in a clerical job, he struggles with depression and feelings of failure, as there is a yawning gap between what "he is" and "should have been".

How do I develop a healthy self-esteem?

Need for self-acceptance: I am okay the way I am.

Where do the notions of "I should have been" come from?

- I should have been 6 feet tall, but I am only five feet five inches;

- I should be witty and outgoing, but I am shy and retiring;
- I should have been an engineer from IIT, but I only managed a diploma;
- I should have a great rapport with my boss, but I am such a '*lassu*'.

They are nothing but society imposing its own norms and standards upon us. Those with a strong self-esteem understand, "The perfect human being has not yet been born. I can never be perfect. No one can be perfect. And I am okay with my imperfections."

You are perfectly within your rights to aspire to change and improve, but remember that goals should be realistic, and in the process of moving towards the future, you don't reject your current self.

Ask yourself what you want, rather than being pushed by others' expectations.

At first Arvind Goswami felt very bothered by the fact that his batchmates after eight years' service drove luxurious cars and bore fancy titles (like Assistant Vice President, General Manager, while he was still Manager). He would feel needled when his wife asked him when they were changing their old Maruti.

However, after a period of introspection and soul searching, he realised that these were not his aims. He was content pursuing his hobbies of collecting prize-winning cacti, being secretary of the Rotary Club, and coming back from the factory in time to be with his children (unlike his friends in senior positions). This is what he explained to his wife, and which she accepted after initial resistance. This acceptance does require courage, but the Goswamis are content today, and their children and doing well.

Ten action reminders to develop a strong self-esteem

1. Dress and look your best at all times. Personal grooming and appearance play a role in creating first impressions—it is a projection of how you feel about yourself inside.
2. Take initiative in volunteering your own name first whenever you

meet someone new, or in telephone calls. By taking pride in your own name, you are communicating your comfort with yourself.

3. When you speak to anyone, look at the person in the eyes (without staring). It is one of the most important non-verbal indicators of self-confidence.
4. Respond with a simple, courteous "thank you" when anyone pays you a compliment for any reason.
5. Don't criticise or speak ill of others. People who are okay about themselves don't need to "win" by pulling others down.
6. Draw up a list of reasons you are grateful for, what your blessings are, what your recent achievements have been. (*Everyone* has an island of competency, an area which is a source of pride. Identify it).
7. Draw out your self-development plan (your own personal horoscope): Your own goals for improvement. Make them specific and time-bound. They can be in areas of professional development, health and personal appearance, relationships or planning your finances.
8. When you experience failure or receive negative feedback at work, tell yourself it is not the end of the world, but a necessary (and inevitable) part of learning and growth. If you feel upset and de-energised with failure, give yourself permission to do so, but only for a limited time (say, one day). After that you have to dust your knees and move on.
9. Focus on what you can learn from the (negative) situation. You may find you need to brush up on your skills or polish up your resume for a new job search. Turn your disappointment into a stepping stone; not a roadblock.
10. Also learn from a success experience. Don't dismiss it as a "fluke" or "luck" or that it meant "nothing". Acknowledge and accept successes, for they are important sources of feedback too.

Coping with angry feelings

When Gopal Patnaik submitted his resignation (with a flourish), his boss Mohit was surprised. Gopal's outward behaviour in the two years that his boss had interacted with him had always been agreeable, even subservient, with his "yes, sir", "right away, sir."

A lack of congruence between our behaviour and feelings sends conflicting (and confusing) messages to the boss.

He had seemed the epitome of loyalty and cooperation.

However, it was in the exit interview that the boss was completely taken aback. Gopal spat out his rage when he said, "Never was I so humiliated and angry when last January you changed my role and put me under Bala Krishna." Indeed there had been a departmental restructuring, but Mohit had no clue that Gopal had nursed such strong feelings!

As a subordinate, many questions come to the mind—Should I bring up this issue with the boss? What can I say? How do I say it? Suppose it is misunderstood? Shouldn't the boss figure out my feelings and do something about it?

Does suppression of feelings help?

No. You may not say anything, but the stomach, heart, blood pressure, etc. keep the score. Every time you interact with the person or think about the situation, the tally increases, until one day there is an ulcer, or acidity, or heart attack. Or an eruption completely out of proportion to the situation. Everyone is taken aback, including you.

Acknowledge and own the anger

A prerequisite is to recognise and admit you are angry. Unfortunately, many of us are taught while growing up that it's "bad" or "wrong" to be angry, and we end up denying these feelings. You may have seen a friend whose face is red, fists clenched, veins standing on his forehead, saying, "Angry? I'm not angry!"

Why judge anger as good or bad? It's just an emotion we experience—and while we are experiencing it, it's real for us. (It may be warranted or unwarranted, that's a separate issue). If channelised, anger can generate constructive energy too. Anger can make us complete unfinished tasks, take on difficult goals, make us even more determined.

Take responsibility for your anger instead of becoming a 'victim'.

Have you heard others (or yourself) say?

- "He really makes me mad..."
- "Everytime we have a meeting, I have a headache..."
- "It's because of him that my day is completely ruined..."

What we are doing is externalising the source of our problem, and therefore handing over power to this person (boss). In other words, it's nothing to do with us, and everything to do with him. Is he the author of our feelings, emotions and well-being? Surely not! Our feelings are generated from within us, by us, and about us. Would everyone in my position react the same way? No. Perhaps another person would be even more scared, a second even more angry and a third, completely indifferent. My reactions are unique; they are me. And only I can have a handle on them. The healthiest and most positive people say, "It is up to me how I respond to this difficult person (or situation) thrown into my life."

Expressing our feelings

Building bridges with the boss means keeping channels of communication open, and never allowing a situation where the boss is taken by surprise. *Congruent communication* means an accurate match between what we are saying and what we are experiencing. Lack of congruence creates its own stress inside us, and also sends conflicting messages to others. The next two chapters deal with how to put across sensitive issues to the boss calmly, dealing only with facts, and putting aside emotions. We may not get the results we want, at least right away, but we have communicated in a respectful and friendly matter our concerns, making it easier for others to understand us.

Staying open to the other's perspective

After expressing our concern, it's important to stay open to the possibility that my anger is arising out of *my* view of the situation, and there may also be another perspective. We may not ultimately agree with it, but we need to accept that reality is not limited to what we experience. So do listen to the other's reply.

Many of our fears and doubts come from our inability to accept ourselves ("I am not good enough"). When we view ourselves critically and harshly, we look at others also with the same "eyes". This is the reason which causes us to judge others severely and critically, making us intolerant and unhappy! If we are able to embrace ourselves—warts and all, and develop skills in being aware of our feelings, accepting and owning them, and integrating them with our intellect and will, we will allow ourselves to learn and grow as individuals.

8

Getting the Manager's Blessings for that Super Idea

"I have so many ideas to market our product—credit cards. For example, many of our Savings Bank customers have credit cards but don't use them. I see so many possibilities and untapped potential of how to activate these dormant cards. But, when I bring them up with my boss, he just drums his fingers on his desk. His replies vary between "It will never work" and "I'll think about it." Six months ago, he asked me to make a presentation of my ideas to the Marketing Director (the super boss), which never saw the light of the day, as I never got the opportunity to present them."

—Abdul Khan, Assistant Vice President, Credit Cards

We all desire to prove our worth—in our own eyes as well as in the rest of the world. We strive to meet both needs—to test our capability and reach maximum potential; and to have it acknowledged by others. This is the drive in us that initiates change and wants to bring new ideas at the workplace. The mistake we make is to anticipate that others are waiting with open arms to welcome these dreams and transformations.

Why do we meet with resistance? What are the reasons that others can't (so easily) see the value of these brilliant ideas? How much of it is because of us—the way we communicate, our ability to make it attractive to an audience, and ownership (mine vs ours) we generate? How much is due to the receptivity (or lack of it) of the superior? Let us look at some of the reasons, and examine whether it's possible that we need to do a better job of "selling" our idea.

Whose need is the idea serving?

If you have an idea, which you believe will work, you have to look deep inside and very, very honestly answer the question, "What is the real reason I want to push this? Is it 'me' or is it the 'organisation'?" In other words, is it my objective to showcase my talent and look good, or is it because there is a genuine benefit for the company? Because, if the driver becomes "I am its author, and don't you forget it", others are quick to sense it, and are not likely to collaborate with you toward its implementation. So ask yourself these vital two questions:

- How will the company benefit?
- How will my boss benefit?

Also, whilst talking to the boss, we need to be aware of the silent messages we are unconsciously sending. If the tone has a ring of oh-so-brilliant-me having to cope with this loopy-jelly custard, you will certainly be sabotaged in your efforts, whatever be the worth of your idea or scheme.

Are you selling from the customer's perspective?

That's right–we need to put ourselves in the boss's shoes, and address the question that every good salesman considers: "What's

If the boss's response is unenthusiastic, don't get bugged; ask questions.

in it for the other person?" In other words, we need to list the benefits from the customer's standpoint.

Let's look at a husband's communication with his wife. On the one hand, he can say, "You know, the office crowd has started playing cricket on Sunday afternoons. I'd like to join them, as it would be a great opportunity for bonding and teamwork. Is that okay with you?" or he can say, "Honey, you've been wanting to spend time with your mother... What if I drop you and the kids there from 3 to 5 p.m., and I'll pick you up after playing some cricket with the office gang. Will that work for you?"

Which is more likely to get him what he wants? The latter, of course. We should never forget that our communication is largely aimed to sell, to influence, to persuade—our point of view. Instead of saying to your boss, "I want more budget", or "This is the only way it will work", talk about how the department will benefit, how the boss's life will become easier, or how it would result in saving money over the next two years.

Don't get bugged, ask questions

When bringing up the idea with the boss, a less than lukewarm response can bog us down. Instead of allowing yourself to get disheartened and giving up, ask questions to draw out your boss's thoughts such as:

- "What comments do you have?"
- "What are your thoughts on this?"
- "What are your views?"
- "Do you think it will work?"

Stop yourself short if you find you have launched into a monologue—the idea is to engage in a conversation.

If the resistance is verbalised in the form of, "No, I don't think this will work", ask more open-ended questions:

- "What part of this doesn't look workable to you?"
- "What are the drawbacks?"
- "You have a lot of experience—what are the gaps as you see it?"

When your boss answers, listen carefully and neutrally to his perspective, and respond to his objections. You could even leave with, "Can I do some research and get back to you in a week's time?"

If your boss says, "Let me think about it", accept it gracefully;

don't pursue it right now. Close the conversation with, "Right, I'll talk to you later about it." Do make it a point to follow it up.

Table 13

A __Alert__ other person.	*Can I have a few minutes to discuss something important with you?* (Try to have a conversation where you will have your boss's full attention).
F Describe the __facts__.	*I notice I bring up a lot of ideas—which I must mention are with the objective of the department reaching its goals efficiently and being seen as the cutting edge department.* (Appeal to shared values—we all want the same results here.)
I __I__ statement expressing your feelings, concerns.	*But somehow I find I have created some barriers, as I am not being able to put my points across well.* (Notice there are no blaming sentences like, "You don't seem to be interested", or "You never respond to my ideas".)
S Put forward your __solutions__, point out benefits.	*Can I request you to give me some feedback? Is it the quality of ideas—are they not practical, or am I loosing sight of some perspective; or is it my style of communicating that is putting you off?*
H __Hear__ the person out.	Be genuine in your intent to seek feedback. (A subordinate once asked his boss for feedback, and thereafter, could not restrain himself from giving counter-arguments in self-defence, pointing out flaws in the boss's logic, etc.)

Are you repeatedly being stonewalled?

If on a recurring basis you find you are not able to make any headway and the boss continues to be apathetic to your ideas—

you could think of actually broaching the subject. It's not something we usually do, but combining the principles of assertiveness (respect for both you and me) and the importance of feedback will open the door for better communication. Given in Table 13 is how the conversation could go using A.FISH.

Garner support from all sides

One of the biggest mistakes in attempting to implement a new idea is to go it alone—as the lone crusader of change in the face of all odds. Indeed, there is a need to engage in an ongoing dialogue with people around, then listen vigilantly to their reactions—which will range from scepticism to, if you are lucky, mild interest. In the process you will gain many things.

One, you will learn the potential flaws. You would naturally tend to prefer to talk to those who are generally known to be positive and receptive, but you must also make it a point to talk to the hardened cynics. They will tear apart your ideas, and if you resist the urge to defend yourself, you will be able to assess the true worth of your idea. Because if after a day, you are still enthused by it, you know you should go ahead. Two, you will get practice in making your brief presentation. Three, in the course of your discussions, if you 'win over' an opinion-maker, a rising star, or someone the boss trusts—your case becomes stronger. While talking to your boss, you can let slip this person's opinion in support of your cause. This is especially useful with low risk-taking bosses (lost-in-the-fog boss as well as agreeable-but-undemanding boss). With them the emphasis should also be on proven solutions or testimonials (Company X-Y is already using it successfully).

Keep talking to your boss too, whether or not he is receptive. Solicit his inputs, and when you are ready, request for a meeting where you can formally present your idea. At this time, the concept should not come to him out of the blue—he already knows what you want to talk about.

Are you ready with your delivery?

Are you able to communicate your idea in a capsule of less than five minutes? If not, there are few chances of your being able to hold your boss's attention, let alone sell it. Let's look at the following example:

Table 14

A Alert other person.	*Boss I would like your advice on the issue of repair and maintenance of office vehicles.*
F Describe the facts I I statement expressing your feeling, concerns.	*Currently, each senior VP's car goes to different garages, and it is becoming very time-consuming to negotiate rates afresh with every garage, and then follow-up to keep track of the progress.*
S Put forward your solutions, point out benefits.	*I would like to suggest we standardise on two garages near our office–which will be convenient to everyone–for all repairs and maintenance of cars. This will enable us to negotiate competitive rates, which will result in savings of about 20 per cent of our budget. Delivery to the senior VPs will also be faster.* (Notice, his not saying this will save me a hell of a lot of bother).
H Hear the person out.	*What are your views on this?*

One of Kannan's responsibility as an Administrative Officer is to ensure timely repair and maintenance of all office and Senior Vice Presidents' cars. Currently, vehicles go to different garages—

as per the Senior VP's recommendation/convenience—requiring time and effort to coordinate on Kannan's part. Kannan wishes to suggest to his Manager to standardise on two select garages. Using the A. FISH framework, he plans his two-minute presentation as given in Table 14.

The receptivity of your boss

After all the effort you make to sell your idea, it could still not make the grade—and the reason could also be your boss's belief in status quo. In that case you have to take your call—either to file those ideas away for the time being in the hope of finding a suitable opportunity, or a different boss in the future, or to whittle away at them s-l-o-w-l-y, making him believe they are his ideas.

On the other hand, there is another option—to actually go out on your own. In a study conducted of flourishing entrepreneurs, 80 per cent said that had they first offered their (now successful) idea to their managers in earlier organisations, which were rejected!

The push to do "something" in life often comes from frustration; it doesn't come when things are going well. So what about checking with yourself if you are willing to put all your eggs into your idea, and take the ultimate risk of quitting and starting your own thing. In a nutshell, are we willing to step away from the safety of our present, to go forward to the unknown which may hold abundant promise?

The answer is 'no' if you don't ask the question

Red tapism and officialdom will always exist in an organisation. Who said it's easy to bring about change? There are three routes you can choose to follow:

- become a closet complainer;

- turn into a pasture-grazing cow;
- live life with passion and energy.

In this last option, you pursue your course with persistence and willingness to take the risk of hearing a 'no'. But you will never know unless you try.

9

Plugging those Communication Gaps

9.1 Clarifying Expectations

"Recently my boss put me in charge of a new project—to set up a customer complaints and feedback cell. The problem was that like any other time, my boss was vague and unprepared with the specifications of the deliverables. When I asked him questions about requirements like deadlines, budgets, etc., he responded on the spur of the moment without thinking it through (which turned out to be quite unrealistic). The project was doomed to failure from the start because of lack of clarity. It was easy for him because he just airily gave instructions. As we rolled it out, there was confusion all around, including between the departments we had to coordinate with—HR, IT, Accounts…."

—Raj Shekhar, Service Delivery Leader

The ideal boss, of course, would not only make expectations crystal clear, but would also ask you for your inputs on what you think should be budgets, deadlines, etc.! But we know the ideal boss is as rare as the leprechaun in China.

Why do we wait for (and not initiate) clarity?

From a young age, we have been conditioned and taught by the society to be cautious. When young children want to play and experience harmless adventure like squelching in the water puddle on the road, running out in the rain, or take decisions like wearing (mismatched) clothes of their own choice, what do they hear? The most repeated words are: "No", "Don't do that", "Come away from there", "What will people say?". Good behaviour, they learn, is to follow instructions and *wait* to be told what to do. Little wonder that taking initiative and risks is all but throttled, and we end up mastering the waiting game.

Why, look at the fairy-tales and stories young children are fed on. Cinderella *waited* to be rescued by the fairy godmother, Snow White by the prince, Red Riding Hood by the woodcutter... so deeply ingrained is waiting in us through culture and upbringing, that we abdicate to our superiors our responsibility for enterprise and resourcefulness.

Answers you need to know

When there in a lack of clarity, why do we shy away from asking questions? The biggest barrier is the fear of looking incompetent in the boss's eyes. Thoughts like, "I didn't want him to think I can't handle it" or "How can I say I don't have the answers?" go through our mind. We need to remind ourselves that being assertive means having the right to ask questions, saying, "I don't understand", or asking for help.

Here are some questions we need to ask:

1. ***Why is the project/task being taken up?***

You may need to dig deep here, beyond the hype of "the MD himself has asked for it". To understand the importance of the task in the context of the whole picture, ask questions like, "What

From a young age we are tought to follow instructions and wait to be told what to do.

are the implications of the task?" or "How will it affect the current operations/systems?" Sometimes you will encounter impatient replies along the lines, "Just get on with the job for heaven's sake", or "Let's focus on getting the show on the road". Don't give up digging until you have clarity—ask others around if your Manager himself is fuzzy about the answers.

2. ***What is to be done?***

In a classic example, the Manager stipulated, "I want a comprehensive report on cost-to-company of employee welfare schemes in our industry. Select a few comparable companies and show me a cost comparison as a percentage of turnover." When the employee came back with the report, a thick dossier of excel sheets, figures and more figures, the boss growled, "What are your recommendations?"

A surprised employee: "I didn't know you wanted any."

Impatient boss: "What the hell am I supposed to do with this *Mahabharata*?"

Make sure you have understood the goal, the task, the results, what you should do and the situation you wish to be in when the task is completed.

3. ***Do I have it in writing?***

For major projects, write down your understanding of the task and have it approved by your boss. This is one way of ensuring your picture matches with that of your boss's.

4. ***Do I have the required resources?***

Sometimes we fall headlong into the task, so anxious are we to get started and to prove ourselves that we forget to pause and take stock. To complete the given task, do we have the physical resources, skills, and proper authority? If the answer is 'no' to any of these, it *must* be raised with the boss. Go to him with reasonable solutions and requests.

At a meeting, a Manager questioned a series of problems reported by a customer. "It's lack of infrastructure," blurted out one of his subordinates.

"What d'you mean?" shot back the boss.

He was surprised (and unhappy) that this was the first time he was hearing of it. Upon probing, he discovered that efficiency could be increased within an upgradation of the machine. It would cost money, but it would be worth it, he assessed. Why wait for a minor crisis, or for the boss to ask, "Is there a problem?" If the employee had brought this up on his own, valuable project time would have been saved.

We suppose that what is obvious to us must be so to the boss, forgetting that he has a myriad other issues to keep track of, and to highlight our issues is up to us. We also box ourselves with assumptions, "There's no point in asking", because we are afraid of hearing a no. But you will never know unless you ask.

5. ***Are deadlines realistic?***

Clarify deadlines of tasks and sub-tasks. If you feel you are being pushed with the dates, learn to negotiate and ask for more time. Bosses do have a propensity of giving deadlines, which need to be completed in the yesteryear. Instead of replying a 'yes' or 'no' immediately, look at the task and calmly figure out how long it would take without being steam-rolled by it. Then go back to your boss with a "counter offer", if required. It is better to face the music now than a far more adverse reaction later when you can't keep the deadline.

Clarifying roles and goals at beginning of year

The same principles apply for putting down goals clearly at the beginning of the year. Many companies insist on measurable and clear goals being laid out, against which performance is measured at year-end. However, the mistake most often made is that these annual goals are filed away and not seen until the year is over. Have you ever experienced disappointment or shock after receiving your boss's ratings (or the results of the ratings—your performance bonus or annual increment)? This is a common enough occurrence, and if the answer is 'yes', you need to do two things: Understand what your boss defines as excellent performance, and make sure you proactively monitor his expectations the whole year.

If you don't have a specific format or system for writing goals, making the effort to do so on your own initiative will pay enormous dividends in avoiding misunderstandings and withdrawal of trust.

The first step in goal-setting is to think realistically about what you can actually accomplish in the year and be held accountable for. As far as possible, bring an element of measurability so that at the time of evaluation, with minimum ambiguity, one can answer: Was the goal achieved? To what extent? With what benefit to the company? Targets should also include some amount of stretch to provide a positive challenge, but they should not be impossible to achieve. If your boss is imposing goals that are too difficult, ask for help in the form of training or extra resources.

Knowing your boss's work-world

In your mind you need to be clear about the priorities of each goal, as seen from the boss's point of view. To answer this question, you need to take the trouble of stepping into your boss's shoes, and finding out:

- What are the organisational goals he is responsible for?
- What is important to him?
- What is getting in the way of meeting his goals?
- How can you help him achieve his goals?

When you discuss your objectives with your boss, indicate priorities and time allocation towards each. Your boss's responses will enable a good cross-check with his perspectives of their importance. Talk about what are excellent results for each goal.

And finally, insist on/ask for/request for regular reviews. Discuss with your Manager, if possible at least once in two to

We need to step into our boss's shoes to understand his world.

three months your progress, difficulties and also what you want from him. Alert him to any changes in track due to altered priorities and keep a diary of the outcomes of these meetings.

9.2 Disagreeing with the Boss

When you disagree with the methods or conclusions of your boss, will speaking about it mean committing career suicide? Most of us swing between two extremes of "cautious silence" and rubbing the boss the wrong way with an attitude of "your battery isn't all there". It is possible however, to take the mid-route of a

The dilemma of "to speak" or "not to speak" when my views differ from the boss's.

candid and civil conversation where controversial opinions are brought up. At the workplace, people with contrary opinions aren't going to go away, and the stakes will continue to be high. Hiding behind your computers or memos won't take your career places.

Don't go to the boss when emotions are high

"As a technical leader, I look after three to four products and am responsible for their quality, maintenance and delivery, feature enhancement, etc. Before going on (a long overdue) two weeks' leave, I discussed the schedule of pending deliveries with my boss.

On return from leave, however, I found that my boss had ignored these schedules, and had aggressively over-committed on delivery dates, which were totally unrealistic. I was so enraged that I stormed into his room, blew my top, and quit."

—*Rajesh Talwar, Project Leader*

Rajesh responded aggressively with, "I'll show him" and "I am not going to take this horse manure any more" ringing in his mind. His anger gave him a false sense of bravado—making him lose his inner balance, and he ended up damaging his own interests. The first rule is: Avoid going to the boss when your emotions are running like a misfired Diwali rocket. Give yourself a cooling off period to collect your thoughts and composure. If Rajesh had used assertiveness skills of A. FISH (Chapter 6), this is how he could have planned the confrontation with his boss:

Table 14

A **Alert** other person	*I have some concerns about our project deadlines. Is this the right time to talk to you?*
F *Describe the **facts**.* I **I** statement expressing your feelings, concerns.	*I know the market isn't in good shape, and we are lucky to have several projects on our plate. I see some problems in our delivery schedules. There are two separate projects due for completion – LK Bank on 31st January, and Micro Grinding on 15th February. There is no way Micro Grinding will get it done on time. If we try to speed it up, there will be slippages and bugs—and one unhappy customer.*
S Put forward your **solutions**, point out benefits.	*Let us talk to both the customers and try to get an extension and see if we can reprioritise and reschedule. The other alternative is to divert resources from internal Information Technology Department to beef up the*

Contd.

	second project. If there were four extra programmers working on Micro G, it would be possible to complete work on time.
H Hear the person out.	*What do you think?*

That part of us which is the most ripped and affronted is our ego. "How could the boss do something so stupid, that too without consulting me," screams the mind. Momentarily we loose perspective of the objective—to find a workable solution.

Put your ego aside and focus on the solution

Ranjan Jaiswal is a civil engineer working with a construction company. He was asked by his boss to install 65 washbasins in a housing apartment complex in the next 24 hours to be ready in time for a public health inspection. This is how the interaction went.

Jaiswal: *It just can't be done. It isn't even possible to ready a plyboard stencil (to cut the marble slabs), as the company carpenters are not available at such short notice.*

Boss: *Then cut the marble without the stencil.*

Jaiswal: *Sir, if you remember, we tried that a year back in the Abhilasha complex, and we had to waste over a thousand square feet of marble.*

Boss: *I don't care how you do it, but complete, it has to be.*

Jaiswal: *With all due respect, sir, I would rather not do it than do it the wrong way.*

That's how the matter ended, with the work not getting done, and of course, resulting in a lot of bad blood between Jaiswal and his boss. Later when Jaiswal was reflecting on the deadlock with a lower temperature, he realised that he had got so caught up in self-righteousness ego—"I am right and the boss is bananas", that the focus on problem resolution got thrown out of the window. There could have been many solutions (if he had maintained his inner balance), including buying a light cardboard or chart paper from a stationery shop and cutting a stencil out of it!

Don't jump to conclusions; ask open-ended questions

We love to arrive at a verdict that confirms our favourite beliefs—that the boss's decisions are as logical and well thought out as the mice that followed the Pied Piper of Hamlin. But we may be missing another perspective here. The decision could have been taken from information basis we don't have access to. From his position, the boss may have to take stock of various other angles, considerations and repercussions.

A team leader in a software development project one day opened his e-mail to find instructions that henceforth every project must be accompanied by the SQL–E2 quality compliance documentation. This was a comprehensive and cumbersome format in which all employees had not even been fully trained yet. It would cause costly delays in their projects.

To the team leader, it was the most absurd diktat passed by an idiotic and brain-dead upper brass. It was easy to pass scathing remarks at the water-cooler, "Don't they think about ramifications before passing out decrees?"

However, if he had suspended judgment, he could have asked open-ended questions like

- "What's the intention behind the mandatory SQL–E2?"
- "How are we going to communicate standardised procedures across all employees?"

He is then more likely to understand the big picture and work collaboratively, than if he were to barge into the boss's room and shoot, "What's the need of the SQL-E2? Where did that come from?"

The team leader learnt subsequently that the company was planning to go for export of their products to new countries, which made this process mandatory.

Homework, homework, homework

It won't help if you go up and say, "This decision will cost a pretty packet and we haven't budgeted for it." To make sense to your management, you will need to speak the same language–calculate in advance costs like development, trials, infrastructure, etc., as well as customer-related repercussions. If this is not your area of strength, don't give up. Take help of someone from accounting or finance. If you are feeling diffident or hesitant in asking for help, you need to check with yourself if you have invested in building a friendly network within the organisation.

Atul Bajaj (Manager, Inventory and Process Control) was at a loss when his newly appointed boss seriously questioned and rubbished his planning methodology. The boss found the ratio of inventory to sales unsatisfactory. The fact *was* that marketing forecasts in the company were very high, and the trend was to be conservative and maintain high inventory levels.

Bajaj realised that the only way to maintain tighter inventory levels to save inventory storage was to question the age-old policy of high forecasts and 'safe' inventories. Easier said than done! However, Bajaj decided to do his homework and get his data in order. He spent four days in preparing mathematical charts and tables to work out modified ways of calculating inventories which would save money, but involved higher risk-taking. He then spoke to his boss, explaining how to neutralise inaccuracies in marketing reports to arrive at lower inventory levels. Using this method would reduce inventory, though risks would go up by 10 per cent.

Bajaj was able to persuade his boss and the rest of the senior management to use the new approach, which worked better for the company in the long run.

Alternatives do exist to keeping quiet and biting your lips when your views differ from the boss's. While it is not easy to put aside angry and hostile feelings, we need to focus on finding the solution rather than 'winning the round', and ask open-ended questions rather than jumping to conclusions. These are skills that can be learnt with conscious effort and practice.

9.3 Difficult and Sensitive Issues: Should I Speak Up?

"I feel so overworked and stretched. In the last two years, my organisation has grown at least five-fold, and with it my work-load. However, there is no corresponding increase in my resources or compensation. I feel this should happen automatically, but nobody really seems to be giving it a second thought."

—Leena Matthew, Assistant Manager, Administration

"Recently I had to meet a difficult deadline for my Manager. I wrestled with it till midnight, and felt a sense of accomplishment when I executed it and handed it in time. Guess what he did–he put it away and didn't look at it for two days! You can imagine how deflated and disappointed I felt. What should I do the next time he gives me an 'urgent' task with a crazy cut-off time?"

—Alok Jaideep, Team Leader (at a Call Centre)

"My boss really micromanages. He gives detailed instructions for tasks I can do on my own, checks progress frequently, and questions every small decision or recommendation I make."

—Tilak Patil, Maintenance Manager (Manufacturing Organisation)

Should I speak up?

In situations like this when emotional sensitivities are high, and it feels so much is at stake, we feel very vulnerable. We are weighed down by anxieties, uncertainties and doubts about our own communication skills. 'Should I speak up or stay quiet? Better to leave things unsaid in case the situation worsens,' we say to ourselves warily. However, chances of the situation improving on its own are very slim, and by not saying anything we end up feeling hopeless and helpless.

According to assertiveness guidelines that we have seen, it is indeed legitimate and required to bring up issues that are pricking us, rather than playing the silent sufferer game. Let us use A.

FISH framework to handle these tough conversations in a calm and respectful manner, without putting ourselves down or loosing our cool.

Take Leena Matthew's situation above. After agonising over the frustration of not being recognised or acknowledged for her work, this employee takes an appointment with her boss. She plans her script or dialogue as follows:

Table 15

A Alert other person	*I'd like to speak to you for 20 minutes about a career-related matter. What would be a good time?* (Your Manager may ask you to sit right now, or fix time to meet later).
F Describe the facts	*I started this job two years ago in Administration where I handled responsibility for housekeeping, security, cafeteria and reception for two offices in Delhi—headoffice and regional sales office. We have since then acquired two more offices in Gurgaon. I am managing the expanded premises with the same staff, and almost the same salary.*
I I statement expressing your feelings, concerns.	*While it has been exciting to meet the challenge of expansion, I do feel overworked, at times frustrated, with the increased running around. As people work late in offices, my staff is stretched—often working 10 to 11 hours a day.*
S Put forward your solutions, point out benefits.	*I do need your help to cope with increased work-load. I need two additional staff–one at officer and one at staff category. This will reduce overtime costs for the company as well*

Contd.

	as improve quality of administrative services. I would also request you to look into an up-gradation in my level with commensurate salary increase.
H Hear the person out.	*What are your thoughts?*

Preparing your conversation also requires anticipating questions, resistance and refusals. If the boss says, "You are right, we have indeed expanded. At the same time we have outsourced housekeeping in two of our locations, which has reduced your direct work-load. Nevertheless, can you show me some data of break up of responsibilities handled and man-hours of your staff required as per today's requirements?"

You should make sure you have data and facts available.

Asking for what you want

To state this directly is often difficult as we are inhibited by self-imposed constraints and self-beliefs like:

- "Who am I to ask?"
- "It is for my superiors to decide."
- "What if they think I am greedy?"
- "They must not think I'm good enough, otherwise I'd have got my promotion by now."
- "I am not ready for promotion yet."
- "I don't deserve it."

But this is submissive self-talk at its best. It has to be replaced by assertive thoughts like, 'I have the right to ask for what I want and to be treated fairly. I have worked hard in the last two years. What I am asking for is a request, not a demand. Certainly it is not a situation of all-is-lost if the answer is no.'

It's okay to ask for what you want.

It's okay to ask for what you want

Jack Welch, CEO of General Electric for 20 years, writes in his autobiography, *Straight from the Gut*, that four years after being with the company, the General Manager's slot fell open and "I went after it". He asked his boss, "Why not me for the job?" His boss's reply was, "Are you kidding? Jack, you don't know anything about marketing. That's what this new product introduction is all about."

Welch didn't take 'no' for an answer. He spoke to his boss for well over an hour, "pounding him with my qualifications for the job, thin as they might be". His boss didn't give him a reply then. Over the next seven days, Welch called him with additional arguments to support his case, and got his promotion.

Table 16

A Alert other person	*Can I have 10 minutes to discuss something important about our way of working together?*
F Describe the facts	*I do understand this is an important and sensitive project we are working on. We have been meeting three to four times a day to review step-wise progress, and I have been checking every decision with you.*
I I statement expressing your feelings, concerns.	*While I feel very supported with your hands-on approach, can I request that I work on each phase, and then bring it to you for approval?*
S Put forward your solutions, point out benefits.	*Perhaps we could meet twice a week on Monday and Thursdays, for evaluating and assessing the situation, and once a week I can write you a detailed status report apprising you of my progress. This should work as I have now been working on similar assignments for the last two years. It would leave you with more time for other projects, and would also help me develop and grow under your guidance.*
H **Hear** the person out.	*What do you think? Could we try it out for a month?*

Something is brothering you: One more example

Let us revisit Tilak Patil's situation as mentioned earlier.

"My boss really micromanages. He gives detailed instructions for tasks I can do on my own, checks progress frequently, and questions every small decision or recommendation I make."

Using assertiveness skills, we can plan to say as given in Table 16.

There are, of course, no guarantees that you will be able to find an ideal solution or work things out to your satisfaction. In the worst case, you may not even get a patient hearing. However, we have seen that thorny and awkward situations *can* be discussed in a calm, inoffensive and at the same time, flexible manner. Speaking about it rather than leaving it unsaid has these advantages:

- Somewhere your requirement will register in the boss's mind even though he may not immediately and outwardly accept or agree.
- You will send out signals of, "I feel confident enough to speak up; I will not be taken for granted."
- Your own self-respect will go up for having spoken ("I tried my best").

10

Bosses who Harass and Terrorise

In the third chapter ('Types of Bosses and How to Deal with Them') we saw four key boss-styles, and some suggestions on how to treat them. Clearly, the most difficult to live with is the bully or abusive boss. One woman described her former boss as an "alpha-shark who called me in daily and screamed at the top of his voice. My stomach would start churning as I reached my workplace, and I dreaded his arbitrary mood swings."

There could be varying intensities of unpleasantness, ranging from thorn-in-the-flesh to tongue-lashings that feel no less than whip-lashings. The victim's self-dignity is left feeling no more than a frozen pudding. It is a difficult situation to walk away from. Quitting is an option that exists theoretically, but in the real world, you have to live with many constraints. Leaving too soon after joining may look bad in your bio-data; another job may not be immediately available; you may feel unsure if these are "setting in" blues, etc. On the other hand, if you stand up to your boss, or talk to someone else in the organisation, there is a fear of a backlash—he may get back to you in some way.

The brutal boss.

So bully bosses push around their subordinates openly and uncaringly because their power overawes and silences their targets. In this chapter we will look at some ways of standing up to the assault. It's not easy, but mentally preparing yourself and then learning to respond in a calm and planned manner with appropriate words and action will strengthen your dignity. No one can do this for you but yourself.

Tough boss or brutal boss?

When a subordinate isn't getting along with the boss, every word and deed of the superior is seen in a haze of suspicion and dislike.

It's easy to get into a blame mode—that the boss is the root of all problems. It's important therefore to differentiate between a negative boss and a demanding boss.

Demanding or tough bosses:

- Communicate their expectations in a forthright manner. They may say: "Here are the targets, and here are the areas I need to see improvements. We will review in three months, and if you don't reach them, here are the consequences."
- Focus on the task rather than the personality.
- Demand that you give your best effort all the time, and require that their standards be met before giving a compliment.
- Criticise the quality of the work you do.

Nasty and brutal bosses:

By contrast, nasty bosses attack you personally, using their power and position to withhold information, demean with tempers flaring up so much that they seem out of control, shift blame in the eyes of seniors, stifle innovation and steal credit.

If you are not sure that your boss's negative behaviour is crossing the borderline into bullying and abuse, look at these questions. If you answer 'yes' to four out of five questions, you may be getting pushed around.

Table 17

1.	When you are criticised, are your faults frequently pointed out, weaknesses pounced upon, and self-esteem eroded? Yes/No
2.	Are you often left with a feeling of being shamed, or discredited, or shown up in bad light at work? Yes/No

Contd.

3.	Is your boss known to have practiced bullying behaviour in the past with other juniors? Yes/No
4.	Is your boss known to shout out his frustrations (on you), reacting with uncontrolled anger, especially when things go wrong? Yes/No
5.	Do your responses to his unreasonable demands leave you feeling weak, powerless and ashamed in your own eyes? Yes/No

An unhelpful reaction

In the previous chapters we have seen several examples of fight-or-flight responses to difficult situations. This emotional hijack is the most common, instinctive (and ineffective response) in the face of stressful situations.

Binoy Thomas had been working extremely hard on an assignment, for 12 to 16 hours a day since the last few weeks. In his understanding, his progress was as per the target and on an even keel. He had been regularly updating his boss through e-mail, and weekly meetings. However, one fine day, his boss stopped by his desk, looked over his shoulder, and sarcastically remarked, "I thought this would be finished by now. This just won't do!"

Something snapped inside Binoy when he heard his boss's (according to him) insensitive and unfounded remarks. Binoy's *fight* response was loud, unexpected and uncontrolled, "Why don't you take over the project? I'm not going to work further on this until I have an explanation for this remark."

There was a shocked silence in which, Binoy recalls, his heart thudded, and then sank to his feet. Even in that heated and confused state of mind he knew "this is not the most appropriate response".

In the *flight* response, the behaviour of the subordinate is like a punching bag—meekly and silently accepting a verbal attack or unfair treatment. Alternatively, he takes the avoidance route—not communicating, brushing issues under the carpet, increased absenteeism, and finally, quitting.

For example, when Puneet Sharma was yet a trainee, his boss expected outputs and results from him beyond the scope of his competence, experience, or for that matter, his role and responsibility. When Puneet asked for more resources or time to learn and then deliver, his boss would taunt and berate him. In all these times, Puneet never replied. He just bore it dumbly and meekly with his eyes lowered.

The first step to inner balance—monitoring my self-talk

When we are faced with a difficult boss, is it possible to access our inner balance? How can we change from a reactive response (of *fight* or *flight*) to a more proactive one?

If you look around, you will see that the bully boss has favourite victims who take a special place in being at the receiving end of his venom. He is not 'equally' nasty with everyone—even among his subordinates. What is it that causes some to be 'attack-prone'? Is their performance not up to the mark, which causes the boss to target them? Not always.

The vulnerability of these sufferers is higher. They are more likely to take the anger personally, allowing it to reflect on their self-esteem and dignity. Their internal self-talk is an over-reaction and distorted: "This is awful. There he starts again, and there goes my career out of the window. My work must be whale manure; I'll never be able to satisfy him. I'm a fool to listen to *his* whale manure, but what choice do I have?"

The boss is quick to sense the symptoms of "ideal prey"—tensed facial expression, a withdrawn silence, collapsed body posture, lowered eyes to hide the flash of angry, embarrassed and helpless resentment. When the aggressor watches his victim squirm, he gets a kick out of the power and hold he has on another human being, and is encouraged to continue his behaviour.

So it is possible that you are 'inviting' this hounding and harassment by your own silent signals of 'come-and-beat-me'. Is it possible to get out of this cycle of self-destruction by strengthening areas of personal vulnerability?

An inspiring story

"*Nobody can make you feel inferior without your consent.*"

—Eleanor Roosevelt

Mohandas Gandhi was a fine example of a person who had mastered the art of maintaining his inner balance. Here is an incident from his life, which illustrates this well.

At the invitation of the British government, Gandhi was travelling to England by ship for discussions and negotiations after he had started the Quit India movement. In the ship was a fellow-traveller, an Englishman who couldn't restrain his disdain and scorn for this half-bald, half-naked, and toothless 'brown-native'. Wishing to express his strong views directly to Gandhi, he wrote nasty things and drew funny drawings on sheets of paper, which he pinned together with a paper clip. Walking arrogantly to the deck where Gandhi was sitting, he handed over the sheets. "Here is something useful and interesting for you. Read it and keep it with you."

Gandhi's eyes did a quick scan of the young man and his presentation, and with his customary calm, separated the clip, keeping it with him, and put the sheets in the dustbin. With a quizzical look at his would-be tormenter, he countered, "I've done exactly what you asked me to do."

It is said that the man had posted a few friends on the upper deck as he had expected some fireworks and special effects as Gandhi's reaction. However, it was he who held his head down as he realised the fathomless depth and wisdom that came from Gandhi's unshakable inner balance.

I also remind you of the well-known story of Gautam Buddha who, in the course of his wanderings and discourses, met a man who resented and strongly disputed his teachings. This man visited Buddha, and let out a volley of angry and offensive words. Buddha remained calm and serene. When he left, a disciple asked him, "Lord, how can you remain so unaffected?"

Buddha replied, "If someone were to offer you a basket with rotten oranges, would you accept it? So also, I didn't accept his offerings."

BLASTS: A four-step model of what you can say to your boss

'Heck, I'm no Gandhi or Buddha. I'm just your average guy next door, and I can't overnight turn into a saint.'

That's probably what's going through your head right now. Sure, its not easy, and it will take effort and practice. No getting away from that. The idea is not to reach Gandhi's or Buddha's stature—but certainly to learn to move from a reactive to a proactive mode will help you at all times with—your boss, your juniors, your customers, even with your spouse, with your children. Isn't that a worthwhile goal, to maintain your equanimity with all these characters in life's drama?

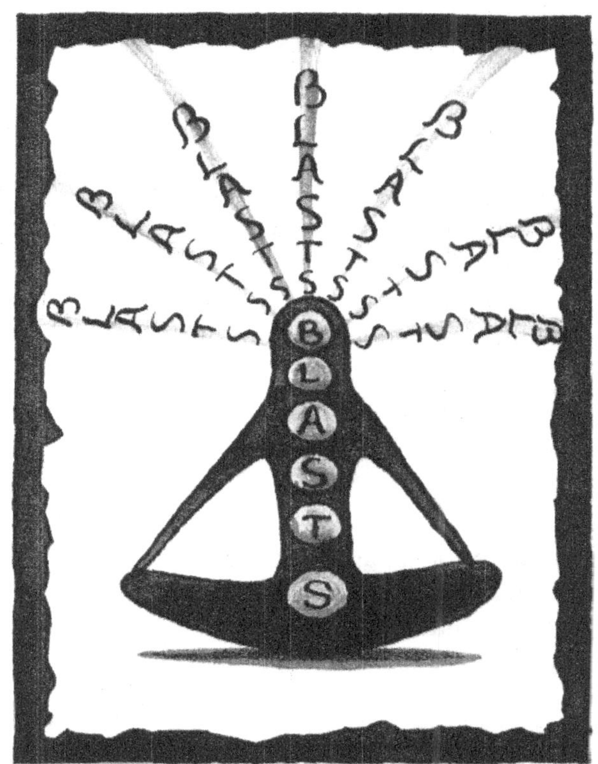

BLASTS: A four-step model of what you can say to your boss.

Let us take the help of the strategy outlined below (BLASTS), and apply it to a real-life situation as a case study.

Raman Juneja's boss asks him to prepare a proposal for a new Employee Rewards Scheme, which Raman submits to his boss. The boss makes his dissatisfaction known in his usual loud, abrasive and degrading manner. "What kind of a proposal is this? Why can't you think through the details and repercussions before submitting it? Where are the cost implications? You are wasting my time as well as yours. You're always bringing me half-baked stuff..."

BLASTS provides you with guidelines on how to react and respond.

Table 18

B	Maintain your inner <u>balance</u> and shift emotional gears. Say to yourself, "I can stay calm. I don't have to take this personally."
L	<u>Listen</u> attentively and unemotionally (easier said than done!). *Hint*: Imagine you are an alien from outer space assigned to study behaviours of unreasonable bully bosses on planet earth!
A	Find something to <u>agree</u> about!
S	<u>State</u> your understanding of his view.
T	Focus back on the <u>task</u>, moving forward with solutions, choices, alternatives.
S	<u>Stroke</u> him in the process, acknowledging his expertise, seniority, etc.

Let us look at each step in detail.

Finding inner balance–Changing our self-talk

The first step is to clearly identify negative behaviour as unreasonable, demeaning and harmful. Learn to shift emotional gears and say to yourself:

- "This is toxic and can harm me. I don't have to accept it."
- "I can maintain my inner balance. I don't have to take this personally. Nobody can take my self-respect from me."

With the help of BLASTS you can face a bully boss more calmly.

- "I'm not going to take this seriously. The boss's views are not about what I am, but what he thinks I am. There is no need for me to feel ashamed and guilty."
- This incident is more a reflection of the boss's problem of not being able to get a handle on his anger. It is not a reflection of my incompetence or inadequacy.

This positive self-talk will help in shifting emotional gears from the old pattern of accepting the toxicity, to now saying 'no', when you are being judged or criticised. Now we are ready to frame a verbal response, which communicates to both—the boss and you, "I am in charge, and while I respect you as an individual, I have respect for me too. I am not going to cower and grovel."

Find something to agree about.

Whenever you are at the receiving end of harsh or judgemental words, look for some aspect of truth in it, and make a statement of agreement. On a lighter side, for instance, if someone says, "What an idiot you are!" you can retort, "I've always thought so myself", or "Luckily, you don't know worse things about me!" It will take the wind out of the critic.

Even if your mind is strongly protesting, "How dare he blow up my report into shreds with his criticism, after the late nights I've spent on it? He has no hands-on knowledge of employee expectations, sitting on his lofty pedestal," resist the urge to defend yourself.

Because the moment you start defending yourself, you are disagreeing with the boss's reality. For him, the reality is that he has found your report inadequate and incomplete and he's feeling impatient, annoyed and probably angry at this time being wasted. We get too attached to our 'reality' and feel that the world will come to an end if we don't convince the other side. But it's a paradox, isn't it? The more you convince, will he get convinced? No. The polarities in fact escalate. So there is a need to give up. Nearly 2,000 years ago, the philosopher Epithets said, "If someone criticised you, agree with them at once. Tell them if only they knew you well, they would not bother to criticise only that!"

So what about acknowledging the boss's reality and starting with, "*I can see the report hasn't met your requirement*", *or "Looks like there are some big gaps here"*.

Listen hard, and state your understanding of his view.

Listen to what he's saying as if your life depends on it.

Everyone has a need that others listen, understand and agree with them. Listening stops when we are full of ourselves. Most people get rigid and stuck to their views because they get frustrated. The reason they get aggravated is that they think—quite rightly—no one is interested or bothered about what they are trying to say.

One way of indicating that we are receptive and paying attention is to briefly summarise the other party's view as well as what we think he may be feeling. This immediately reassures that you are "with them" and tuned in. This is called empathising, which Daniel Goleman, author of *Emotional Intelligence* defines as "understanding what someone feels without their having to tell you."

Next would follow, "*What I hear you saying is that the criterion for the rewards distribution isn't clear, and the cost implications have to be built in.*"

Focus back on the task, and stroke him in the process.

You could say, "*These are important dimensions, and I'll incorporate them and revert to you by tomorrow at 2 p.m. If possible, can I request for 10 minutes of your time today as I'd like to cover these aspects a little in detail? It would be really value addition for me.*" (*Tip*: Don't apologise, and don't show you are afraid of him).

Your response, taken as a whole, would sound like this:

"Looks like there are some big gaps in the report. What I hear you saying is that the criterion for the rewards distribution isn't clear, and the cost implications have to be built in. These are important dimensions, and I'll incorporate them and revert to you by tomorrow at 2 p.m. If possible, can I request you for 10 minutes of your time today, I'd like to cover these aspects a little in detail? It would be really value addition for me."

Let us take another example. Going back to Puneet Sharma's

situation and using the BLASTS model, this is what he could say to his Manager.

BLA : *You are right, I am largely doing a routine but high volume job of sourcing and hiring candidates.*

S: *You're saying I need to do something beyond this.*

TS: *Your idea of developing the Oracle database system is fantastic. If I spend two hours every evening, say 4.30 to 6.30 p.m., it would take me a fortnight to put it in place. Is that okay with you?*

Be proactive: Pre-empt your boss's questions

When Arjun's boss called him to find the status of his assigned project, Arjun knew he was in trouble as he was behind schedule. Arjun's team had developed the new software product for their client, but its installation at the client's site was still pending, as it was awaiting upgradation of machine.

How do you think his boss reacted when Arjun replied, *"I realise the urgency of task completion. It's almost finished; a part is left. I have solved the problem, which was hampering our progress. I'll take it up as soon as possible."*

The boss was understandably infuriated, *"What do you mean as soon as possible? This is the stupidest and most vague answer I have ever heard. What have you been doing so far, sitting on it? What about some specific dates..."*

Arjun was thinking, 'How can I be specific because I first need to speak to the client and get his commitment on when he'll upgrade his machine?'

Arjun made the mistake of not being hands-on and quick enough to have spoken and got the client's assurance before speaking to his boss.

In conclusion, bully bosses are a reality of our work world. They can cause damage to our personality by their demeaning and demoralising behaviour. Needless to say, the first step is to ensure our performance and delivery is a step ahead of their expectations. When their attacks are unreasonable and unprovoked, we must make sure we don't get mired in self-blame, shame and guilt. By following the BLASTS model, we can learn to face their onslaught with greater equanimity.

11

How to get Noticed (and Promoted) at Work

I have been with my organisation for the last seven years. I know I am a good team player as I get along well with my colleagues. I am technically sound—one of the best in my area in fact. But recognition always seems to pass me by. In meetings, my suggestions are ignored, later I find them being taken up for implementation. In other words, I fail to 'get noticed' or 'get credit' for them. The unkindest cut of all was when a newcomer with half my technical expertise was promoted into a position I was hoping to get. What does it mean to me? Why was I the victim of partiality? What do I need to do to become more visible than the fly-on-the-wall?

—Ratan Goel, Project Manager (Software Company)

The situation is familiar enough for you to recognise someone around you who fits the bill, isn't it? It could be a colleague at the next table, a best friend, or more painfully, yourself. This is the story of Muthuswamy (whom we met in Chapter 1), and Muthuswamys exist in every organisation. The saving grace of Ratan Goel is that instead of crying at the boss's unfairness and wrongness, he is willing to look at himself and his style of managing the situation. His question is, "Should I be doing something different? What is that?"

How do people get promoted?

This is a question that has baffled and eluded employees across all work cultures and environments, including denizens of the corporate world. To find answers, a study was conducted by Harvey Coleman (who has worked with America's leading corporations, including IBM and Xerox) across a number of large organisations. Most people are taken aback with the survey result. It has far-reaching consequences as it defies many of our closely held notions and beliefs about the 'real' workplace.

What determines promotion besides performance?

According to the study, there are three factors that determine promotion:

1. **Performance**: Are you on top of your work? What is the quality of results you turn out? Do you get things done? How reliable are you with deadlines? Or, in other words, how well are you delivering on the job you were hired for, as well as beyond it?
2. **Image**: What impression do you create about yourself and your job? Is your boss fully clued in about how good you are? When you produce stellar results, do you keep your bosses informed?

   What is the attitude you wear at work? Have you let it be known that you enjoy your work, and whenever required, are willing to take on an unpopular assignment to make life easier for your boss? Do you do this with a smile and a laugh? Or, do you work hard but remain under immense pressure and (others get the feeling) you view challenges as a burden?

   Are you known for boundary-less behaviour—extending cooperation to colleagues or do you switch on the charm only when you need something from others?

We need to manage our performance, image and exposure to climb up the ladder of success.

3. **Exposure**: In an organisation you work (indirectly) for people other than your bosses too. Do these decision makers, i.e. people at the top who have a say in your promotion know your face, your name and your work? You may be delivering results but if the right people don't know you exist, you won't move up.

   This means building alliances within the system, raising your profile, telling people that you exist, you're good, and what you want.

So far so good, now here comes the unexpected part—the bombshell, if you will. The study also assigned percentage values to each of these three factors to indicate their relative importance in 'how people get promoted'.

- Performance contributed to 10 per cent.
- Image contributed to 30 per cent.
- Exposure contributed to 60 per cent.

It sounds unfair and unbalanced, doesn't it? The huge effort we put in achieving outstanding results contributes to only 10 per cent towards getting us promoted.

Many people react with disbelief or dismay at these figures, and go into either of the two reactions. One is *denial,* "I would never try to prop up my image and exposure. It is all about manipulation, and against my value system", or "I don't agree with these figures. At least, it doesn't happen like this in my organisation". It's okay if you don't agree cent per cent with the above figures and argue with the percentages, but look at the overall message coming through—can we still deny the existence of these other two factors in our lives—'image' and 'exposure'?

The other is feeling overwhelmed by a sense of *helplessness*: "I don't have any of these skills. I didn't see my father doing it either in his career. Even if I wanted to, I would not know how to."

Let us look more closely at the two mysterious entities—'image' and 'exposure' and understand what it takes to manage them.

11.1 Enhancing My Image—Creating the Right Impression

Do you feel uncomfortable or queasy at the thought of 'selling yourself' or blowing your own trumpet? Are you one of those who believe in 'my work should speak for itself'? It's not about projecting an image of what you are *not,* but about portraying what your abilities *are.* Underplaying them will not get you anywhere.

If you are a hard worker and a good employee, but don't feel like you are on the radar screen of top management, you need to gain a higher profile for the good work you do.

Here are some points to keep in mind:

1. Demonstrate competence: Show initiative and be a thought leader

One of the best ways of standing out, or 'shining in white space' as workspace experts have labelled it, is to take on additional responsibility outside your job description and comfort zone. If you see a problem at the workplace (which you may not be responsible for, but is affecting your efficiency in some way), take ownership of it (be a thought leader) and offer to solve it. Or take up a tough assignment which others are unwilling to take on. Or take on a task that makes life for your boss easier, like doing some number crunching for the next budget.

Service delivery leader Kannan, in charge of accounts payable process noticed that different locations of his business had different standards of accounts reconciliations. The number of accounts reconciliations a person did in one location was 100, in another 300, 250 in the third, etc. On his own initiative, he developed a matrix to standardise and improve the processes.

In another example, when his boss had to prepare a pitch for key overseas visitors about operations review, Raghu offered to do it for him. Realising Raghu had a good grasp of what was to be done, the boss asked him to also stand and deliver the presentation. For Raghu this was a good exposure to senior brass.

Needless to say, you have to put in effort and extra hours. The important thing is to treat these as opportunities rather than a burden if you have to accomplish something that your boss (and others) will value and notice.

Of course, don't go overboard in putting a finger in every pie, and take on so many projects that leave you overburdened. Limit yourself, choose your activities carefully and focus on doing them well.

2. Build rapport with your colleagues–don't hide behind your computer

Technical people spend so much time on their technical affairs that they don't give importance to communicating and building rapport with colleagues. The disdain for the latter comes from either 'technical arrogance' or sheer ignorance of the fact that to influence others, to win support for ideas, or participate in key projects it is critical that co-workers think well of you.

In your organisation do you see people who demonstrate a helpful spirit and an understanding attitude? When asked to provide extra technical support to another project or department, do you consider it an opportunity, rather than a burden?

Do you also see some colleagues who are self-centred and dismiss others as stupid? They turn on their charm when help or support is needed. Do you recognise them? Just as we are quick to pick up subtle clues, so also do others sense where we are coming from.

3. Be well informed

To be known as the 'go-to-person'—to whom people go for a problem, build a reputation of a SME (subject matter expert). Watch market trends closely by reading journals and interacting with peers in the industry. You should be able to predict the next technology in your field, and then teach yourself the necessary skills. Jasmeet, a financial-sector IT professional, pushed the case to his boss of starting a new web-based trading system, only as he was fully in the know of the technology and design behind it.

It's not enough to be competent—you must be perceived as competent.

Develop a specialist area of expertise so that you are recognised as an authority in the subject—so that even the boss comes with questions to you.

4. Its not enough to be competent–you must be perceived as competent

"My colleague is always yapping about her achievements, be it at meetings or at the water-cooler in a chance encounter with the boss. I find it obnoxious, but the boss thinks highly of her. Guess, who puts in all the hard work? That's right, me. Shouldn't a good boss be able to see through the drama and hype she creates?"

—Gurmeet Singh, Production Manager

No doubt your ability to produce excellent results is of utmost importance, which includes skills in problem solving, thinking through implications of decisions, bringing new deals, exceeding targets. But, if there are two employees with ***comparable levels of performance***, who is the likely candidate for promotion—Muthuswamy, who hardly speaks at meetings, keeps his eyes lowered, and answers in monosyllables; or Juneja who through his articulation and expression conveys an exuberance, confidence and passion for his job?

- *Talk to your boss* about successful completion of a challenging project, or the way you solved a problem, or any achievement, be it sales figures, or a brochure ready ahead of time and under the budget. It gives a good feeling and builds self-esteem.
- *Making a monthly summary of top five achievements:* It is a good idea to document your output to keep track of how you are contributing to the organisation. It helps in three ways: One, it focuses your own efforts in reminding you of your goals, the direction in which you are heading and how you are utilising your time; two, it reminds you to keep your boss informed and maintain a healthy and necessary flow of communication; and three, during the annual performance appraisal meeting you will be ready with your homework. Don't expect your boss to remember everything that you did in the year!

Talking about own achievements

Sometimes we get bogged down by a mind-set, "If I speak about my successes, I'll feel silly, a sham." It's nothing but a thinking bind because of our upbringing, where we have been taught as children the value of undermining and underplaying our talents, which we call 'modesty'.

Amongst two (or more) employees with comparable levels of performance, the candidate with higher visibility is more likely to be considered for promotion.

There are however, deeper issues involved—of low self-esteem and internal messages of 'you are not good enough' which make us feel uncomfortable to talk about our own accomplishments and feats. It is time to challenge old notions and understand there is nothing wrong in projecting what you are—you are not presenting what you are not.

How to say it?

Here are two examples of actual words used by two different employees. Which rings convincing, positive and self-assured?

Muthuswamy: *"The new masala-noodle launch-and-distribution was finished just before time and within the budget."*

Juneja: *"I'm really proud that the new masala-noodle launch-and-distribution I worked on (or my team worked on) was completed before time and within the budget."*

Juneja's statement sounds more positive as it actively connects him with his achievements, while Muthuswamy sounds more passive.

Contrary as it sounds, all this can be said without sounding boastful, if you can convey modesty and humility in your tone, and acknowledge other team members wherever appropriate.

5. Ensure face-time with the boss

"I agree communication with the boss is vital...but I don't even get to see him. He is so very busy...he gives me barely ten minutes a month, and he has a limited attention span. After five minutes he starts looking at his watch and then his laptop."

—Rajat Ganguly, Service Delivery Leader (BPO)

Perhaps the boss is truly a busy and important person. Perhaps he doesn't manage his time well, who knows? Some bosses are hard to pin down.

Rajat Ganguly was asked, "How does your boss behave with his other subordinates? How do they cope?"

The reply was, "Some of my colleagues actually camp outside the boss's door (find a reason to be there) in the morning and evening when he enters or leaves the room and try to grab some minutes of face-time. He asks them to ride with him as he is driven to the airport, or walk with him down the building to the car park, or travel to the next meeting (and return by taxi). I wouldn't do it because at my level I think it's demeaning to do so."

So there you are. Others are managing more interaction time with the same boss because they realise its importance; they do not have ego hang-ups and are flexible.

When you ask for a meeting with your superior, think through carefully what you will say, ask and do. Peter Drucker gives an old rule: "It takes ten minutes of preparation for each minute of interview time." If your boss prefers it this way, send a note in advance with a formal agenda. You must have your own prioritised check-list to make sure you cover all your points.

5. Anchoring: Leaving a positive feeling in your boss's mind

Have you noticed that when you think of certain people, or on meeting them, or on learning of their presence in a forthcoming meeting, you privately flinch or recoil. They create an unpleasant sensation in your unconscious mind.

You have to be careful that you don't create a negative emotion in your boss's memory. Even if you have a disagreement, or you have not got what you wanted, make sure you leave on a positive note. Your facial expression, body language and tone should convey a gung-ho, upbeat tone rather than sulking, going in a huff, or feeling sorry for yourself. Similarly, don't be known as a cribber and complainer. As author Dale Carnegie says, 'Any fool can criticise, complain, condemn, and most fools do.'

11.2 Exposure: Enhancing Visibility

"I'm just not getting the right exposure to my seniors and my immediate boss is to blame as he should actually be projecting me."

—*Ritika Kumar, Senior Software Engineer*

Why is it important to be noticed by senior management? What do I have to do for it to happen? Surely it's not in my hands, as we have to conform to the hierarchy in the system? Shouldn't my boss make my work visible at the next level?

Even while these are valid questions, we do know, don't we, that the final decision about our promotion does not rest with the immediate boss alone?

Yet we get caught up in 'shoulds' and 'musts' ...(the boss *should* be more perceptive, *must* provide the right exposure...). Our 'musts' and 'shoulds', will not change things. The bottom line is that we have to learn how to make ourselves visible to other decision-makers in the organisation. The harsh truth is that no one else will do it, and it won't happen by burying our nose in a *Unix* manual. It's true that without the boss's recommendation, we won't even be considered for promotion. But if we have taken care of exposure, we are making it easier for the boss to sell our case to his seniors.

How to get noticed by senior management?

While senior-rank officers in your company may not spend much time with you, occasional opportunities of brief 'face-time' do present themselves. The question is how you acquit yourself in these moments.

Let's say the senior Vice President-HR is addressing sales officers during their annual sales meet over a one-hour session, followed by a tea-break. What is the usual scenario? The senior VP finishes his tea hurriedly—there are usually one or two people (mostly the organisers) who try to make conversation. The rest straggle around in self-conscious clusters, keeping a safe distance from the senior person. They are losing precious face-time opportunity simply because they don't know what to say.

Most people don't engage in a conversation with the Operations Head (or CEO, or CFO, or General Manager, or

Managing Director) if they encounter them in an elevator, at the corridor, or in the pantry where you are reaching for coffee together, or while waiting in the cafeteria queue.

The senior may nod at you, or ask, "What's happening?" In these two minutes do you have an informative, lucid, coherent, impressive two-minute speech ready? Or are you 'struck dumb' and answer in monosyllables?

You may well ask, "How can they judge me over a five-minute exposure?" Senior leadership is well experienced at forming reasonably accurate impressions based on snapshot cues. On the basis of the words you use, your tone and tenor, facial expression, they form and carry impressions. Their ability to judge accurately is based on a lifetime of observations; they have also been in similar situations many times.

The two-minute elevator speech

There are two views about it—one set of fast-track corporate climbers who swear by being 'prepared' with a two-minute elevator speech. Prior thought is given to what will be said in the case of a chance meeting with three or four key decision-makers. They don't rely on the-spur-of-the-moment thinking. On the other hand, there are those who dismiss this concept with, "How can you rehearse this sort of thing? Isn't it taking things too far?"

But the point is, it is better to be over-prepared than under-prepared.

What can you say at a two-minute elevator speech?

- A recent company initiative, and the response it has received, e.g. "The idea of recruiting part-time employees with an older age profile at our call centre has really picked up well...the attrition rate at A-B unit has stabilised at X per cent..."
- Talk knowledgeably about a special area of interest of that particular

person, e.g. a finance officer found that his VP was interested in large ERP systems which interact with each other. When he got the chance, he spoke about what it would mean to upgrade, change, implement new systems, how existing systems worked, etc.

- Facts and figures of your own department, your role in it, how it is impacting the bottom line, your joy and excitement in being involved with it, etc.

Are you a mouse-at-a-meeting?

You could be attending a meeting where higher-ranking people are present. Do you speak up? This is also an important opportunity of showcasing who you are by the way you communicate. Which of these three behaviours do you exhibit?

- *Not speaking at all at a meeting*: If you are a mouse at a meeting, you will not be noticed. Usually being struck dumb results from being overwhelmed by the presence of an authority figure. It's not considered a good sign, as one of the desired managerial competencies is to be able to keep your wits about you, even in stressful situations.
- *Being a blabbermouth*: If you are repetitious, or state the obvious, or restate others' points as your own points, you are not making a notable impact.
- *Making sensible and relevant contributions*: Do you bring up relevant, sensible, intelligent, value-added points? What you say must be appropriate and pertinent. The following example will illustrate this point well.

Exposure is a double-edged sword

A batch of trainee Accounts Officers at a large MNC was to be addressed by the Chief Financial Officer. It was a rare opportunity to interact with the senior-most layer in the organisation. Towards the end of the meeting, the CFO asked, "How are things going? Any problems?"

One accountant spoke at length on what a miserable time he was having—the administrative support was lousy as getting a computer set-up had been a herculean task, getting stationery indented was so difficult, there were hassles with company transport, lunch coupons at the cafeteria.

The other officer speaking about his current assignment said, "I have been assigned the cost accounting project at our Noida plant and am coordinating with the GM (Finance) there. I am having serious chemistry problems with him, but I know I have to deal with it, and I'll manage. Now that I have an opportunity with you, I would like your inputs on the project I am working on—how I can make it better." He then proceeded to describe the project briefly, and took down notes as the CFO gave his inputs.

The CFO remembered the names and faces of both officers—so we can say both had exposure. The first stayed in his mind as a whiner and nitpicker who was unable to get beyond petty everyday issues. The picture he formed about the second person was that he had a reasonable maturity level [in fact, the CFO was aware that the GM (Finance) at Noida plant was known to be a difficult person to get along with], was able to differentiate between relevant and irrelevant issues, and keep a handle on what he needed to focus on.

Eight months later the CFO noted that this youngster had done an extremely good job on the project, despite his difficulties with the GM (Finance), and nominated him for a foreign assignment, which had come up.

So when you speak, what do the senior-level managers consider while judging you?

- The *perspective* you are capable of looking at—the level of the problem you bring, the plane at which your mind is settling.

At the junior level one is naturally concerned about whether "journal entry 56 was passed or not", or that Ramaswamy from tax department is not cooperating. Is the person capable of rising beyond this, and *begin* to attempt to look at the boss's perspective as well, the new accounting software that needs to be put in place, controllership problems, etc.

- The *attitude* that you carry with you.

Exposure alone is not sufficient

Exposure is the necessary prerequisite before a superior can form a judgment, but spotlight alone does not guarantee that the impression will be positive. A subordinate who gains exposure increases chances of equally good or bad impact. But without any limelight, you are an unknown entity.

Exposure is like getting a role in a movie or a drama; depending on how you play your role, you will receive accolades or flak. Or it can be likened to getting a place on the race track—how you will actually perform is another story.

Other ways of raising your visibility

- ***Build a support network in the organisation*:** Find out who are the decision-makers and influencers. Build alliances and links with them by, for example becoming part of a multi-disciplinary task force, teaming with different departments to pool resources/ save the company money, etc. Use every company event, new project, and meeting to upgrade learning and keep in touch with people.
- ***Ask a senior executive to become your mentor,*** if possible. In other words, develop a support network of people you can go to for advice and support.
- ***Facilitate training sessions*:** Whenever R. Lal, Finance Manager, was asked to take a training session, in the annual orientation programme for new promotees, he regarded it as an intrusion in his schedule, and went through great lengths to dodge the harried

HR executive trying to co-ordinate the programme. At the last moment, he 'delegated' it to a subordinate.

His colleague, on the other hand, Legal Secretary, Phanasgaonkar, prepared well. His sessions were interesting and participative and he acquired the reputation of a professional who knew his subject well. When the Management Committee had to handpick executives to attend a prestigious Executive Development Programme at their headquarter, his name featured at the top.

- ***Play a larger 'civic' role in the company*:** With already heavy workloads, most people are loath to commit time to organising events like the departmental picnic, charity drives or the inter-location cricket match. But if handled with efficiency and gusto, they help in visibility.

Asking for promotion or raise

Let's say you are doing all the right things—you have exceeded your targets, and helped the boss exceed his. Yet you feel dissatisfied with your compensation as it is below what you think you deserve. Or you are overdue for a promotion.

- Are you going to bring it up?
- Should you take it up?
- How to bring it up?

The very thought of raising the subject with the boss gives us the jitters. We are not comfortable pushing for rewards or talking about how good we are. But an organisation is a mercenary entity—it is in its best interest to extract the maximum with minimum cost. If an employee says nothing, it will be assumed that all is well, and if he continues to perform, he must be motivated.

Your main objective is to deliver a message

Don't plan to expect an immediate response or commitment from your boss. Your main objective should be to deliver a message rather than a demand—that the company should reconsider your salary, or that you feel ready for increase in responsibilities, change in assignment, etc.

Even being turned down may not necessarily be a bad thing. If you receive criticism, treat it as an eye-opening feedback. Listen carefully and decide what to do with it later. Ask questions like, "What needs to be done to get a raise (or promotion)?" Aim to chart out a roadmap—what you need to do further/ differently in the next eight to 12 months. If a pay raise is out of the question, explore negotiation of benefits.

Make a business case

When we face a selection interview for a new job, don't we do a hard sell? We talk about our feats and accomplishments in a planned and systematic manner, aiming to convince we are the best fit. Once we have the job, why do we stop doing it?

Plan the discussion, making a business case out of it, taking out the personal factors and focusing on business issues. Outline real and visible achievements and their impact on the bottom line.

Research your market value in advance as part of your homework. Find out what people with similar background and skill currently earn in jobs comparable to yours.

Consider the situations from the boss's perspective and anticipate objections/ questions. If you are asking for a promotion, how will the department benefit? Will the team need to be reorganised?

Watch your tone

The tenor of your conversation must never become confronting. Nor should you come across as demanding. Position yourself as interested in your development and growth; nor should you place an ultimatum before your superior.

Timing

It is best to either wait for appraisal time, or at the most, ask for an interim one. Another good time is after you have delivered outstanding results on a high profile project, or when you have been given additional responsibilities. The worst time is when the business is facing an economic or market downturn.

While the above establishes and confirms what we had suspected all along, it's a career jungle out there. The good news is that survival skills (if they don't come naturally) can be learnt and mastered; it's not something you have or don't have. Now that we have understood the importance of 'image' and 'exposure', we can take charge of these areas in our lives. The assumption is that we are adept and proficient at our jobs, and firing with all our cylinders.

As we network with peers, seniors and juniors, enhance our image, become more assertive and self-confident, we will see our ability to influence and persuade to go up—in turn, helping us become more effective at our job.